D0073301

Peace in the Post-Reformation

Christians are supposed to love their neighbours, including their enemies. This is never easy. When feud and honour are common realities, it is even harder than usual.

This book sketches the history of peacemaking between people (not countries) as an activity of churches or of Christianity between the Reformation and the eighteenth century. The story is recounted in four countries (Italy, France, Germany and England) and in several religious settings (including Roman Catholic, Lutheran, Church of England and Calvinist). Each version is a variation upon a theme: what the author calls a 'moral tradition' which contrasts, as a continuing imperative, with the novelties of theory and practice introduced by the sixteenth-century reformers. In general the topic has much to say about the destinies of Christianity in each country, and more widely, and strikes a chord which will resonate in both the social and the religious history of the West.

John Bossy is Professor of History, University of York. His many publications include *The English Catholic Community, 1570–1850* (1975), *Christianity in the West, 1400–1700* (1985) and *Giordano Bruno and the Embassy Affair* (1991) which shared the Wolfson Prize.

Peace in the Post-Reformation

THE BIRKBECK LECTURES
1995

John Bossy

CAMBRIDGE
UNIVERSITY PRESS

PUBLISHED BY THE PRESS SYNDICATE OF THE UNIVERSITY OF CAMBRIDGE
The Pitt Building, Trumpington Street, Cambridge CB2 1RP, United Kingdom

CAMBRIDGE UNIVERSITY PRESS
The Edinburgh Building, Cambridge, CB2 2RU, UK   http://www.cup.cam.ac.uk
40 West 20th Street, New York, NY 10011–4211, USA   http://www.cup.org
10 Stamford Road, Oakleigh, Melbourne 3166, Australia

First published 1998

Printed in the United Kingdom at the University Press, Cambridge

Typeset in Monotype Fournier 12.5 / 14.75pt, in QuarkXPress™   [GC]

A catalogue record for this book is available from the British Library

Library of Congress cataloguing in publication data
Bossy, John.
Peace in the Post-Reformation / John Bossy.
p.   cm. – (The Birkbeck lectures; 1995)
Includes index.
ISBN 0 521 64061 x (hardback). – ISBN 0 521 64605 7 (pbk.)
1. Peace – Religious aspects – Christianity – History.   2. Counter
– Reformation.   3. Reformation.   I. Title.   II. Series.
BT736.4.B675   1998
261.8′73′094—dc21   98–24990 CIP

ISBN 0 521 64061 x hardback
ISBN 0 521 64605 7 paperback

FOR

C. C.

Et in terra pax hominibus
bonae voluntatis

CONTENTS

PREFACE

The Mill Lane lecture rooms in Cambridge are full of voices, and it was very agreeable for an undergraduate of the early 1950s to have the chance of adding one more to them in the autumn term of 1995. Those who were kind enough to come and listen will find that the four lectures have been heavily rewritten since. But I have continued to think of them as lectures, and if some of them are now a little long for an hour's talk, they may make amends for the one which turned out to be ten minutes too short. I am very grateful to those who entertained me so nicely at the time, and especially to the Master of Trinity, Sir Michael Atiyah, to Patrick Collinson, Boyd Hilton, Peter Burke and Ulinka Rublack. This is also the moment to remember those whose gifts and tips have enabled me to deal with my subject less scantily than I should otherwise have done: Simon Ditchfield, Eamon Duffy, Steve Hindle, Amanda Lillie, Daniele Montanari, Adriano Prosperi, Mary Stevenson, Marc Venard, Danilo Zardin. Despatches from Italy have been particularly numerous and particularly welcome, and I hope I have done justice to them in the first lecture. More thanks to Libby Walker, who has turned my spotty typescript into an elegant printout; to Linda Randall, the copyeditor; and again and especially to Amanda Lillie, who put me in the way of finding the Sansovino statue which appears on the cover.

John Bossy

Italy

At the beginning of these four lectures I should like to thank the Master and Fellows of Trinity who have done me the honour of inviting me to give them; and to remember two previous lecturers. One of them is Outram Evennett, who gave his lectures on the Counter-Reformation in 1951, and the other is Denys Hay, whose series on the church in Italy in the fifteenth century came twenty years later.[1] In brilliance and coherence, in learning and humanity, not to say eloquence, they are a hard pair of acts to follow. Their shadows will loom. I shall be less optimistic than Evennett, and less pessimistic than Hay; which is partly because I shall be talking, most of the time, about something a little different from either. Meanwhile I express my gratitude to Evennett for the bird's eye view of the Counter-Reformation without which I doubt if I could have got the subject into historical focus at all. These lectures may be found to complement his or to contradict them; but they will always be somewhere around. To Denys Hay I owe a more particular thank-you for introducing me to that magic moment in the history of the West when Duke Giovanni Maria Visconti of Milan ordered, in vain, that the word *pax* be left

---

[1] H. O. Evennett, *The Spirit of the Counter-Reformation* (Cambridge, 1968); Denys Hay, *The Church in Italy in the Fifteenth Century* (Cambridge, 1977; given in 1971).

out of the mass and the word *tranquillitas* put in instead.[2] 'Et in terra tranquillitas.'

My original title was 'Moral Tradition and Counter-Reformation', and it will do for the first two lectures. I put no spin on the second term, and have only to say that I shall be using words like 'reform' sparingly, if at all. On the Catholic side at least, and from where I shall be standing, we can readily get on without them. 'Moral tradition' is a coinage of my own, with some reference to Alasdair MacIntyre's *After Virtue*.[3] It joins together three items: the notion or practical instinct that to be a Christian means to love your neighbour, and in particular your enemy; the fact that in these times and places it was very likely that people might be in a state of enmity towards others, which would call for arrangements of peacemaking if it was to be resolved; and the historic or perhaps archaic connection between these arrangements and the sites, rites and persons of the church. The connection might come in various forms; in so far as it was with ecclesiastical persons, it was very far from exclusive.[4]

That is my moral tradition. Since the term is not self-explanatory, I have substituted for it in my title, 'peace'; but I shall use it throughout these lectures. I take what it represents to have been rather deeply embedded in the consciousness of the populations of the West at the time of the Reformation, and want to know what happened to it thereafter. First, what happened to it in some of the lands where the Roman church maintained its sway; but also what happened to it in lands that became Protestant, which has seemed to me, as I have proceeded, an increasingly

---

[2] Hay, *The Church in Italy*, p. 82 (1409).   [3] 2nd edn (London, 1985).

[4] I have pursued this theme in 'Blood and Baptism', *Studies in Church History*, X: *Sanctity and Secularity*, ed. D. Baker (Oxford, 1973), pp. 129–43; 'Holiness and Society', *Past and Present*, no. 75 (1977), at pp. 130–5; in my edition of the essays in *Disputes and Settlements: Law and Human Relations in the West* (Cambridge, 1983), and in other pieces cited below.

substantial part of my story. Hence the rest of my title, which has the extra benefit of putting due weight on the state of affairs, on both sides of the confessional fence, as the seismic upheavals of the sixteenth century settled down into everyday continuity. I shall say now, so as not to have to repeat it, that I do not see any of the branches of the western church as they emerged after the Reformation as having a special claim to be the vehicle of my moral tradition. At the end of the lectures I shall enquire whether one of those branches had a bias against it.

A few other remarks before I begin. I shall not be asking why people got to hate each other; and I shall be dealing with parties who were roughly on a footing of equality. The focus of my interest, because I think it was probably the centre of gravity of the moral tradition at this time, will be the middle and upper reaches of more or less rural communities. I shall try not to get too involved with the particular case of human relations between Protestants and Catholics as such, or between different kinds of Protestant: it is sometimes important to the main theme, but more often, I think, presents a temptation leading out of the way. I shall take the four countries I discuss separately, because there is a different story in each, and because sometimes I shall need to put the politics back in. Finally I ask your indulgence for having chosen a topic which is both unmanageably large and perhaps rather novel: I feel that it is still in a very plastic state, and that its final shape and import remain uncertain.

It is proper to start with Italy, because Italy has been a favoured environment of the moral tradition. That tradition here had a special force, and was constitutive of a great deal of social and political life. In the back country of Liguria, now classically described by Osvaldo Raggio, law and government amount to the peace in the feud: pacification and arbitration between those in a state of *inimicizia* (enmity), with compensation to *parenti*, who may be natural or artificial, for offences. The instrument, one may say, of continuing existence is the *instrumentum pacis* drawn up by, and lodged with, the notary. Churches have altars where such *paci* are celebrated: in the plainest case, Our Lady of the Miracles, no less. The kiss of peace is exchanged; marriages may follow, projecting amicable relations or new hostilities into the future. Here the priests of the parish or *pieve* are not involved, except as parties, since every one of them represents his *parentela*: the notary, the local grandee, the visiting commissioner of the state, which is the Genoese Republic, are the arbitrators. Virtually nothing to do with the clergy, the peace process is nevertheless – possibly all the more – a work of Christianity. It is also essential to everything else. I quote Raggio: 'The political unity of the group of kinsmen is built . . . above all on enmities, their settlements, and the *paci*.'[5]

You will say: the back-blocks of Liguria are the back-blocks of Liguria, not the Po valley, or Venice or Milan. But what we have found there is a model of what prevailed throughout the peninsula and its appendages, and not only in the mountains and the islands, though it stood out more starkly there, and had less competition. The moral tradition, of which Liguria offers a particularly functional example, throve in mountain and plain, city and countryside, north and south. At the highest levels of Renaissance sophistication we may think of it as weakening; the state, which holds the ring in Liguria, will act more directly in Tuscany. Such things will matter in the long run: they had not yet disturbed the centrality of this tradition in the moral consciousness of Italians. Italy was the homeland of the fraternity, one of

---

[5] Osvaldo Raggio, *Faide e parentele: lo stato genovese visto dalla Fontanabuona* (Turin, 1990), introduction and chaps. 1, 4, 7, quoted at p. 177; the only comparable study that I know is Otto Brunner, *Land und Herrschaft*, 4th edn (Vienna and Wiesbaden, 1959), pp. 1–110.

whose marks was the settlement of disputes among members; of friars like San Bernardino, endlessly preaching the social miracle to vast crowds in fifteenth-century cities; of the real and fictional Piovano Arlotto, whose pursuit of charity and good humour in and out of the *Uccellatoio* (the Fowlhouse, an inn at Macioli outside Florence) made him a classic representative of the moral tradition and the hero of a best-seller of long standing which the Counter-Reformation failed to suppress. It was home, to finish, to the now equally but tragically famous miller Domenico Scandella *alias* Menocchio, who thought, if I understand him, that the Gospel could be reduced to the words 'Forgive us our trespasses.' He was not the only one.[6]

There was plenty of confusion in the peninsula during the fateful decades between the emergence of Luther across the Alps and the closure of the Council of Trent, and one of the things subject to confusion was the status of this moral tradition. I am not thinking here of Machiavelli's radical scepticism about the utility of Christian ethics, but of confusion in the ranks of those from whom the counter-reformation church was to emerge. I illustrate it, briefly, from the career of Gianmatteo Giberti, split by the dreadful sack of Rome in 1527 between his European politics as Pope Clement VII's secretary of state, dedicated as much as Machiavelli to the 'liberty of Italy', and his ecclesiastical government as bishop of Verona, from then until his death in 1543. The first part was a fiasco, the second inspired a generation of successors. He was an intensely vigorous and, his doctor said,

---

[6] Ronald Weissman, *Ritual Brotherhood in Renaissance Florence* (New York, 1982), pp. 1–105; Iris Origo, *The World of San Bernardino* (London, 1963), chap. 6; G. Folena (ed.), *Motti e facezie del Piovano Arlotto* (Milan and Naples, 1953), nos. 36, 64, 143, etc.; F. W. Kent and Amanda Lillie, 'The Piovano Arlotto: New Documents', in P. Denley and C. Elam (eds.), *Florence and Italy: Renaissance Studies in Honour of Nicolai Rubinstein* (London, 1988), pp. 347–67; my *Christianity in the West, 1400–1700* (Oxford, 1985), p. 64; C. Ginzburg, *The Cheese and the Worms* (London, 1980), pp. 11, 87–8, 108–9.

choleric man, and displayed both characteristics in each phase of his *curriculum vitae*: in his impatience to 'renew the world' he had pursued Charles V with unrelenting enmity, and his episcopal mode was not very different. He was not, he claimed with some complacency, a 'bon compagno'. He was held by many, including another personal enemy, Pietro Aretino, to be a tyrannical destroyer of the good old ways of Italian Catholicism, the creator of a system of social espionage, a bringer of discord and hatred into the city of Romeo and Juliet. Aretino was no great advertisement for his cause, but we need to think about it: it launches a number of themes which will return in due course.[7]

Giberti was certainly conscious that peacemaking was one of the duties of a bishop; he may not have thought that he was very good at it, since in Verona itself he gave the job to one of his canons, the cathedral organist.[8] Like most people in the sixteenth century, when he set down what he meant by charity he put the settlement of enmities at the end of a list of works of public beneficence.[9] He made the momentous innovation of the *liber pro descriptione animarum*, later *status animarum*, which he told his curates to keep. This was a nominal roll of those in their charge, with a record of whether they had fulfilled their obligation of Easter confession and communion: a list of those who had not was to be kept and used to enforce conformity. This surgical intervention laid open the heart of our matter, since enmity was one of the two principal reasons for absence from communion: the other was sexual or marital trouble, which is not in itself

[7] Adriano Prosperi, *Tra Evangelismo e Controriforma: G. M. Giberti* (Rome, 1969), especially chaps. 2 and 4; on Aretino, *ibid.*, pp. xvi, 105–6, 292–3; Barry Collett, *Italian Benedictine Scholars and the Reformation* (Oxford, 1985), pp. vii–viii, 112–13, shows that Aretino was no traditionalist, just an enemy of Giberti.

[8] A. Fasani (ed.), *Riforma pretridentina della diocesi di Verona: visite pastorali del vescovo G. M. Giberti, 1525–1542* (3 vols., single pagination, Vicenza, 1989), p. xcix.

[9] Prosperi, *Giberti*, pp. 265–6, 205–6 (formula of visitation).

our business. A party who was 'out of charity' with another, who would not abandon what were called the signs of rancour, might not have his sins absolved or participate in the rite of 'common union', the Lord's supper. Giberti's sanction for non-communicating was severe: public excommunication by name, by the priest at mass, meaning not simply exclusion from the sacraments but expulsion from church and social ostracism, and expressed in the most aggressive terms ('cutting out putrid members'). The time offenders were given to come round was, at least at the beginning, no more than a week or two. I quote Adriano Prosperi: 'With the institution of the *liber animarum* as an instrument for continual recourse to a severe practice of excommunication, the settlement of disputes and irregular situations was entrusted definitively, no longer to the sacrament as a vehicle of moral economy, but to ecclesiastical authority [as such].' Giberti added to the grounds for instant excommunication irreverent behaviour in church and standing outside during mass.[10]

Strictly interpreted, this programme would, as Giberti's enemies complained, have left the diocese after one of his visitations in a state of social trauma. When he began to visit in person, in 1530, he toned it down somewhat, proved more amenable to the recommendation of priests for delay, and distinguished between sexual irregularities and problems of *inimicizia*. In the limited time he had available when visiting three or four parishes a day, he did use his authority to act as a peacemaker. So his bark was worse than his bite; but it was his bark that was transmitted to posterity.[11] There is also a central point of theology that may be

---

[10] Fasani, *Visite*, introduction, pp. cx–cxii, cxxiv–cxxv; text, pp. 93, 372 (time), 499, 636, 794 (language); 669, 681 (church behaviour), and *passim*. Prosperi, 'Le visite pastorali del Giberti', in *ibid.*, p. lvi, quoted.

[11] These are my conclusions from Fasani, *Visite*, pp. 447–828, which record Giberti's personal visitations from April to November 1530: peacemaking, pp. 553, 562, 584, 657, 742, 808 and *passim*. Prosperi, *Giberti*, p. 261.

relevant to Giberti's work. He himself was not what is called a 'spirituale', a person who, like his colleague Reginald Pole, had taken on board the doctrine of justification by faith alone; but many of his team of helpers could be so described, and one of them was his preacher and popular educator Tullio Crispoldi. Crispoldi published a commentary on 'Forgive us our trespasses'; the Veronese may have had, as I do, some difficulty in following him, but he appears to have interpreted the text as a quixotic gesture by God to accept what was intrinsically a matter of civil convenience as worthy of his grace; an incentive to devout contemplation of God's generosity and to a life of other good works. This sounds more like Ockham than Luther; but it touches on two influences which are fundamental to our story, the pull of Reformation theology and the push of Renaissance civility. It embodied what Giberti had said when preaching, and I take it to reveal a good deal of uncertainty about the moral tradition.[12]

It is not usual to diagnose uncertainty in the doings of the Society of Jesus, whose operations were getting under way as Giberti's were finishing, and that is not exactly what I have to propose. The Society will have a part in the story, and often a positive one: surprisingly, to me at least, because I had not thought, and Evennett's analysis of the Jesuit ethos had not suggested, that it had peacemaking much on its mind. One had underestimated the flexibility of the institution and its founder; nevertheless, this may be one of the cases where flexibility borders upon incoherence. Ignatius was a 'spiritual' in his own way, which was not the way of the Lutherophiles or of Erasmus, but the way of a fifteenth-century *dévot* whose favourite reading was the *Imitation of Christ*; and I see nothing wrong in making a distinction in

---

[12] Crispoldi's *Alcune ragioni del perdonare*, cited in Ginzburg, *The Cheese and the Worms*, p. 40.

fifteenth-century piety between the devotional and the social.[13] The activism with which Ignatius transformed the *devotio moderna* was an activism of works: works of charity, works of mercy. A programme of works designed to help 'souls' to a salvation which was to be achieved by infusing the church's sacraments into converted individuals did not focus attention on charity in the sense of the moral tradition. There is nothing about it in the Spiritual Exercises or the original documents of the Jesuit 'institute', little or nothing in the pre-history of the Society. In its mode of life and its dealings in the world, the ties that bound were simply not its thing; in Ignatius's meditation on that part of the Nativity story which recorded a second crux of the moral tradition (after the Paternoster), the angels say: 'Glory to God in the highest', but do *not* say: 'Peace on earth to men of goodwill'.[14]

Peacemaking first appears in the expanded version of the *Formula Instituti* of 1550, ten years after the foundation: here, *dissidentium reconciliatio* (reconciliation of those at dispute) is put down as one of the works of charity the Society exists to promote.[15] It seems pretty clear what had happened. Early Jesuits sent out on preaching tours in the towns and villages of central Italy had found themselves invited to arrange the public cere-monies of peacemaking which would have been expected to occur in the preaching tours of the friars. They had come to flush out Protestants and sympathisers, to teach catechism, to preach penitence and confession; they meant, one way and another, to generate interior conversion. They found that what amounted to

---

[13] 'Prayers', *Transactions of the Royal Historical Society*, 6th series, 1 (1991), p. 138; cf. the remarks of Virginia Reinburg, pp. 148ff.

[14] *The Spiritual Exercises of St Ignatius Loyola*, para. 264 (in the translation by T. Corbishley, Wheathampstead, 1973, p. 87); Evennett, *Spirit of the Counter-Reformation*, p. 36.

[15] John O'Malley, *The First Jesuits* (Cambridge, Mass., and London, 1993), pp. 165–71.

conversion for most of their hearers was the visible reconciliation
of public hostilities, the throwing down of weapons, the kiss of
peace. The principal voice in favour of accommodation to the
demand was that of Silvestro Landini; it was well received at
headquarters, I guess as an orthodox and popular alternative to
the preaching of virtual justification by faith which had been the
message of the *spirituali*. Thereafter, as Jesuits continued to serve
as 'missionaries' to what they thought of as an indigenous Indies,
peacemaking became a standard item of their work and propa-
ganda.[16] But it may be significant that Landini's is not a famous
name in the conventional annals of the Society, for there is a problem about Jesuit peacemaking, which is not really a 'work' in the
same sense as their other enterprises. It got under the wire as one
of the spiritual works of mercy, two of which, converting the
sinner and instructing the ignorant, were central to Ignatius's
inspiration. But peacemaking is not actually one of them: they
include the patient bearing of wrongs and the forgiveness of
injuries, which are something else. If we take it in under this rubric
we need to remember that mercy 'is distinguished from love and
kindness, as connoting in its object a certain inferiority . . . It
excludes the idea of equality between giver and receiver.' It
drops, indeed, as the gentle rain from heaven, but upon the place
beneath.[17] Peace, as we are to understand it here, is not at all like

---

[16] Adriano Prosperi, 'Il missionario', in R. Villari (ed.), *L'uomo barocco* (Bari, 1991),
pp. 211–18; and *idem, Tribunali della coscienza. Inquisitori, confessori, missionari*
(Turin, 1996), pp. 551–5, 568ff (where he is called Cristoforo: were there two of
them?); David Gentilcore, '"Adapt Yourselves to the People's Capacities":
Missionary Strategies, Methods and Impact in the Kingdom of Naples, 1600–1800',
Journal of Ecclesiastical History, 45 (1994), pp. 269–96.

[17] O'Malley, *The First Jesuits*, pp. 88, 166. I have failed to find any historical account
of the spiritual works of mercy, which seem to be a late mediaeval compilation.
H. R. Mackintosh, art. *Mercy* in J. Hastings, *Encyclopaedia of Religion and Ethics*,
VIII (Edinburgh, 1915).

this. It is much more like a marriage, and even according to the Council of Trent the priest did not make a marriage: the parties made it themselves. I do not think I am making a meal of what may seem a purely theoretical difficulty. The Jesuits' adoption of a peacemaking role in this special context was an event of importance for the persistence of the moral tradition in counter-reformation Italy, and perhaps elsewhere. We shall have to see whether it entered the genes of the Society as a whole.

The Council of Trent had nothing to contribute to our story except a supremely vague proposal that bishops on their visitations should exhort the people to 'religion, peace and innocence':[18] it was generally deaf to suggestions that the sacraments, or indeed the church, were social institutions in any respectable sense. It did indeed get a lot of bishops into dioceses, with what result for us I now enquire. We must start with the most memorable of those bishops, Carlo Borromeo, whose nineteen years in the field, running his archdiocese of Milan and supervising the activity of a string of other bishops, are bound to occupy the centre of any story about the Italian Counter-Reformation. As a saint, he is well known: virtually teenage cardinal-nephew and secretary to the amiable Pius IV; convert of the Roman Jesuits; dour ascetic, living on bread and water in his palace; champion of Lent in the battle of Carnival and Lent; saviour, more or less, of Milan in the plague of 1576. As a working bishop he is much less familiar, for all the hundreds of pages of normative matter in his *Acta ecclesiae mediolanensis*, and their subsequent fame; acres of his compulsive paperwork have still to be ploughed through,

---

[18] Session XXIV, *De Reformatione*, chap. 3. I think the word here means 'tranquillity'; it is only to be encouraged by 'exhortation and admonition'; and it does not appear to be regarded as a moral problem, since it comes, in third place, after orthodoxy/heresy and 'bonos/pravos mores'.

and he may well become more, not less, inscrutable as more is known.[19]

Twenty years ago I took the simple view that, in his work and that of his colleagues, 'the motive of imposing Christian ethics on social behaviour had lost ground to the motive of imposing conformity in religious observance'. Comforted as I am by Adriano Prosperi's convergent opinion, I ask myself now whether that was a fair judgement. A bird's eye view of Borromeo's episcopate will suggest that it was. St Ambrose was not the model of a peace-making bishop, and Borromeo's variety of holiness was not that of the holy man above the *mêlée* which we owe to Peter Brown. His early biographers do not make much of him as a peacemaker, except for a case in the city of Vercelli, just before his death. His model was hard-edged, enacting Christian *disciplina* by a mass of episcopal *ordini*: a command economy of salvation. He regarded with impatience or plain hostility most of the institutions with which traditional Catholicism had sought to create a Christian sociability: fraternities of *disciplinati*, church feasting, dancing, carnival. He would have responded differently from Archbishop Antonino of Florence to the claim of the Piovano Arlotto that by making friends in the *Uccellatoio* he had secured more than one *pace*.[20]

---

[19] Biography by A. Deroo, *Saint Charles Borromée* (Paris, 1963); many good things in J. M. Headley and J. B. Tomaro (eds.), *San Carlo Borromeo* (Washington, 1988). I have used Federico Borromeo's edition of the *Acta ecclesiae mediolanensis* (Milan, 1599), except in one case (see n. 31).

[20] 'The Counter-Reformation and the People of Catholic Europe', *Past and Present*, no. 47 (1970), p. 56; above, p. 7; Peter Brown, 'The Rise and Function of the Holy Man in Late Antiquity', *Journal of Roman Studies*, 61 (1971), pp. 80–101; Folena, *Motti e facezie del Piovano Arlotto*, no. 36, p. 65. Lives: A. Valier, *Vita Caroli Borromei* (Verona, 1586) (nothing); C. Bascapè, *De vita et rebus gestis Caroli . . .* (Ingolstadt, 1592), p. 369 (people submit things to his *arbitrio*); G. P. Giussano, *Vita di San Carlo Borromeo* (Brescia, 1613), pp. 72, 440 (Vercelli, done at the request of Gregory XIII); but cf. F. Molinari, *Il Cardinale Teatino Paolo Burali e la riforma tridentina a Piacenza* (Analecta Gregoriana, LXXXVII, Rome, 1957), p. 342.

Almost wherever one can see his personal input, the effect seems discouraging to the moral tradition: the notion of the clergy as a hierarchical order of angels who ought not to get their hands dirty; the ecclesiastical law seen as a coercive criminal jurisdiction punishing moral offences like adultery; the hectic pace of his visitations; the invention of the confessional-box, which still seems to me the illustration and agent of an unsocial idea of sin and forgiveness.[21] His obstruction by the walls of the confessional of the priest's act of reconciliation, the *impositio manus* (laying of the hand) on the head of the penitent, was indeed symbolic of unenthusiasm about social rituals.[22] We can add to it his reform of the *pax* in the mass. The Ambrosian or Milanese rite, which he put a lot of effort into defending, contained a rich celebration of the act. After the Paternoster and the *Libera nos*, with its prayer for 'peace in our days', the priest says to the congregation: 'Offerte vobis pacem' (Offer peace to one another). He then kisses a cross he has made on the altar, or a crucifix in his missal, saying to himself: 'Pax in caelo, Pax in terra, Pax in omni populo, Pax sacerdotibus ecclesiarum. Pax Christi et ecclesiae maneat semper nobiscum' (Peace in heaven, peace on earth, peace among all the people, peace to the priests of the churches. The peace of Christ and of the church remain always with us). When he lifts his head, he gives the peace (a light embrace with a touching of cheeks) to his deacon, and says: 'Receive the bond of peace and charity, that you may be worthy of the most holy mysteries [the eucharist].' Which is what the Sarum rite says as

---

[21] Adriano Prosperi, 'Clerics and Laymen in the Work of Carlo Borromeo', in Headley and Tomaro, *San Carlo Borromeo*, pp. 115, 130; Bascapè, *Vita*, pp. 357–8; my 'The Social History of Confession in the Age of the Reformation', *Transactions of the Royal Historical Society*, 5th series, 25 (1975), pp. 21–38; on ecclesiastical jurisdiction, Agostino Borromeo 'Archbishop Carlo Borromeo and . . . the State of Milan', in Headley and Tomaro, *San Carlo Borromeo*, pp. 85–111.

[22] My 'Social History of Confession', pp. 23, 29.

well. All this Borromeo cut out, leaving only the laconic 'Pax tecum' (Peace be with thee) of the Roman rite and inserting, where appropriate, an episcopal blessing from on high. Giovanni Maria Visconti, he who had wanted to remove the word *pax* from the mass and replace it by *tranquillitas*, could hardly have wished for more.[23]

I should say that Borromeo was influential in diffusing the instrumental *pax*, the object, in Italy and elsewhere;[24] and that a sturdy defence has been offered for Borromeo's intentions, at least, as a peacemaker. From his early days in Rome he can be found commending peacemaking as a spiritual work of mercy; I have said that I do not think this was a very satisfactory idea, but it shows willing. He also, in his synods and otherwise, encouraged or required the erection of peacemaking fraternities: not brotherhoods in the traditional sense whose members would keep peace among themselves, but bodies of notables who were to undertake the function as a general work. The most ambitious of these was the Confraternità della Concordia, set up in Milan in 1571. It was to operate, at least partly, on the basis of anonymous informations, to be received in a box and entered in a register; it would call on the unpaid services of lawyers in securing arbitration. The rules envisaged it as spreading throughout the diocese, in town and country, and as paying attention to those, especially the poor, who would not pardon offences unless they received satisfaction in cash. It was to collect funds for the purpose.[25]

[23] Pierre le Brun, *Explication . . . des prières et des cérémonies de la Messe* (4 vols., Paris, 1726), II, pp. 212–15; Archdale A. King, *Liturgies of the Primatial Sees* (London, 1957), pp. 445–7; above, n. 2.

[24] *Enciclopaedia cattolica*, IX (Vatican City, 1952), p. 499 (*pace*).

[25] Angelo Turchini, ' "A beneficio pubblico e onor di Dio." Povertà e carità nella legislazione e nella pastorale della chiesa milanese', in D. Zardin (ed.), *La città e i poveri: Milano e le terre lombarde dal Rinascimento all'età spagnuola* (Milan, 1995), pp. 191–252, at pp. 196–7, 201, 211, 230–8.

The last point, as well as a sensible concern about intra- as well as inter-family feud, show that Borromeo wished to get to grips with real life. I do not think he succeeded. Angelo Turchini, who has presented the evidence and promises more, puts *inimicizia* down as a 'moral misery' to be dealt with in the same way as poverty, ignorance or sickness, and I imagine that he is representing Borromeo's own view.[26] But it was not a moral misery: it was a moral alternative. And what on earth were anonymous denunciations, as of heretics or witches, doing in the scheme? I can hardly imagine anything more likely to increase the incidence of neighbourly hatred. The scheme seems almost constructed so as not to work, as it indeed appears not to have done: Borromeo's successor found that it was not doing its job even in its own parish (S. Maria della Fontana), let alone in the far-flung diocese.[27]

That left Easter communion and the *status animarum*, on which Borromeo followed Giberti, except that he took a cue from the Council of Trent and substituted for excommunication the lesser 'interdict': meaning prohibition of entry into any church and refusal of Christian burial. The curate, at Easter, was to tell his people that all who did not communicate within the octave would be *interdetti*; during the week, he was to pursue the 'due offices of charity', or go and talk to them, to persuade recalcitrants to come. If they did not he was to publish them, next Sunday, by name. 'Per qualche buon fine' (For some good end), if he thought fit, he might put publishing them off for another week; a third week was only permitted with licence from the vicar-forane (rural dean) and for grave cause. Anything longer

---

[26] *Ibid.*, p. 211.
[27] *Ibid.*, p. 236 n. 112; A. D. Wright, 'Post-Tridentine Reform in the Archdiocese of Milan under the Successors of St. Charles Borromeo' (Oxford University DPhil thesis, 1973), p. 178: 'a more active search was to be made for discords and strife in the parish, settlement of which was the confraternity's object' (? 1586, perhaps later).

was a matter for the bishop.[28] The timetable and heavy-handed threat behind it were quite inappropriate for cases of *inimicizia*, whose resolution must be a 'buon fine' which might entitle people to a week's respite. If this were all, we should have no difficulty in dismissing Borromeo's claims as a peacemaker. It is not, though you have to look hard to find the qualification or contradiction which emerges from the instructions for his vicars-forane on page 700-odd of the *Acta ecclesiae mediolanensis*. The vicar-forane may allow a curate to give an *inconfessus* for enmity until the Feast of the Purification (2 February) 'per poter in quel tempo trattare qualche pace' (so as to be able in that time to negotiate a peace). That is to say, the parties have the best part of a year to settle; after that, if one of them is still *inconfessus*, or if he has confessed but not communicated, he will be *interdetto*. The second case is quite common: I think it means that an expression of willingness to forgive will allow the person to be absolved, but without a proper formal *pace* he will not be willing to communicate. The time allowed here is generous indeed: the only other mention of a reasonable timetable I have seen puts the Assumption (15 August) as the deadline.[29]

I can only (and shall soon) speculate on the reason for the discrepancy between the two sets of rules, and report what I know of Borromeo's practice from his 'apostolic' or papal visitation of the diocese of Bergamo (1575), and from odds and ends of information from his own. It leaves a mixed impression: instructions to enemies to come to concord in ten days, a curate stopping in the middle of mass on the Sunday after Easter to run out of church a

---

[28] *Acta ecclesiae mediolanensis*, p. 720; Prosperi, 'Clerics and Laymen', p. 121.
[29] *Acta ecclesiae mediolanensis*, p. 796; M. Grosso and M.-F. Mellano, *La controriforma nella arcidiocesi di Torino* (3 vols., Rome, 1957), II, p. 208. On peace and non-communicating see David Sabean, *Power in the Blood* (Cambridge, 1984), and below, chap. 3; an example in A. Roncalli and P. Forno (eds.), *Atti della visita apostolica di San Carlo Borromeo a Bergamo (1575)* (5 vols., Florence, 1936–57), II/2, p. 19.

man *inconfessus*, he said, because of a lawsuit. But in a large parish near Bergamo, with a good, learned, old-fashioned priest and birds' nests in the church, A is *inconfessus* for enmity with B, and C *incommunicatus* for enmity with A. A has eventually confessed and communicated on 1 January; the priest, I suppose, has been quietly doing his job of reconciliation. Borromeo does not rebuke him, but tells him to put in a confessional-box and get the birds' nests out. Elsewhere he makes gestures of vindictive rigour and gestures of generosity, which perhaps increase as time goes on.[30]

The signs are divergent, but I shall be rash enough to offer a conclusion. One of the most famous items in the *Acta*, and one into which he put his intimate feelings, was the *Memoriale* which he wrote for the Milanese after the plague. The theme of the *Memoriale*, expounded with unusual eloquence and at unusual length (seventy-five folio columns), is how people should behave so as not to provoke God's wrath in future. San Bernardino, even Savonarola, would have pointed to the sin of *inimicizia* as bearing a good deal of the responsibility; Borromeo simply left it out. The real sins of the Milanese were their pleasure in spectacles, games, dressing-up, dancing and carnival. In the more practical *Ricordi*, issued at the same time and for the same purpose (twenty folio columns), peace and concord occupy about three inches; they are among the things heads of households are to instil into their children and servants.[31] This seems almost as off the point as encouraging anonymous denunciation of feuders: it was the adults who needed persuading. Such misjudgements fortify my conclusion

---

[30] Roncalli and Forno, *Atti*, I/1, p. 315, II/3, pp. 126ff; D. Zardin, *Riforma cattolica e resistenze nobiliari nella diocesi di Carlo Borromeo* (Milan, 1983), pp. 15ff, 62–3, 101; M. Franzosini, 'Clero e società locale nel secondo '500: la ristrutturazione borromaica in una pieve della Brianza', *Nuova rivista storica*, 70 (1986), pp. 275–300.

[31] *Acta ecclesiae mediolanensis* (Lyon, 1683), pp. 1045–220 (*Memoriale*: not quite as long as it looks because the printer went straight from p. 1099 to p. 1200) at pp. 1046, 1048, 1076 etc.; *Acta ecclesiae mediolanensis* (Milan, 1599), pp. 1075ff, 1084, 1106 (*Ricordi*).

that Borromeo did not think very hard about peacemaking, or see it as having much to do with the sacred. He legislated about it because he legislated about everything; and if he had not been so at odds with the civil authorities in Milan he might well have put it down as a civil matter.[32] In practice he seems to have placed it uncomfortably in between: something it was his duty to attend to, but altogether a distraction from essential matters of holy discipline and active charity.

Borromeo's companions and subordinates may be divided into the hard and the soft, the dry and the wet. On the dry side we have the absentee bishop of Trent, Ludovico Madruzzo, whose visitations and other activity date from 1579 onwards: no great figure in himself but the object of a particularly scrupulous investigation.[33] Madruzzo's deference to the old philanthropy seems entirely formal, and there is no allowance for peacemaking in his rules about *inconfessi* and non-communicants. At the visitation the curate is told to send a list of these to the episcopal establishment promptly at the end of Easter week: those who have been admonished 'time and again' and failed to respond are to be publicly *interdetti*. 'Time and again' sounds reasonable, but is a one-off concession: in future years this was to be done instantly on the Sunday after Easter. If interdict does no good, the priest will report the offender to the episcopal curia, who will proceed against him as a heretic; he is also to be *bandito* by the civil authorities. Except for the last, which reflects the position of the bishop as a prince of the Empire, these were the usual rules: they caused heart-searching for a number of the parish priests, who agreed with their parishioners that *inimicizia* was a different kind of thing from heresy or adultery, and looked for a *pace*. They asked

---

[32] Cf. Turchini, ' "A beneficio pubblico . . ." ', pp. 203, 235.

[33] Cecilia Nubola, *Conoscere per governare: la diocesi di Trento nella visita pastorale di Ludovico Madruzzo* (Bologna, 1993), pp. 401–19, 517–19, 531.

for more time. Officially, the answer was no: enmity was not a special case. In private a vicar-general who knew his territory recommended 'a decent extension of time', but told the priest to keep quiet about it.[34] I suspect that resistance by local clergy to the guillotine-effect of the *status animarum* was rather common, and accounts for some of the dither we find in Borromeo's *acta*.

No dither in the acts of Carlo Broglia, archbishop of Turin in Piedmont from 1592. Broglia thought that dioceses should resemble 'well-organised armies, which have their generals, colonels and captains', and his view of the peacemaking process may be gathered from his intervention in a case of gang-rape in 1600. It had been settled by financial composition, arranged by the *podestà* and a local nobleman. Everybody tried to keep it from the ears of the archbishop; but he found out, and sent in troops to arrest the main culprit. They were defeated in their first encounter with the family; but eventually the man was arrested, tried and condemned in the archbishop's court, to what punishment I do not know. In this cowboy story one may sympathise with either side, but Broglia will not have helped to keep the peace of Piobesì, where it happened.[35]

Perhaps it is unfair to draw a contrast with two other bishops who have both been candidates for canonisation, one successful. Paolo Burali was bishop of neighbouring Piacenza during the first half of Borromeo's episcopate at Milan; his rigour was tempered by something more humane. Prosperous as the city was as a financial centre during the sixteenth century, it was notably feud-prone, and Burali put peacemaking high among the concerns of his preaching, his visitations and his advice to his parish priests: the population remembered him for it at his

[34] *Ibid.* pp. 406–11.
[35] Grosso and Mellano, *La controriforma nella arcidiocesi di Torino*, III, pp. 216, 270.

beatification. He recruited Borromeo to help with cases of feud among the nobility; they were not especially close, and it is a tribute to Borromeo's objectivity that Burali was his first preference for the papacy on the death of Pius V in 1572.[36] Alessandro Sauli was a devoted follower of Borromeo who went off bravely to be bishop of the undistinguished see of Aleria in Corsica in 1570. Corsicans had earned their reputation as practitioners of the feud; and Sauli was a man 'whose sense of the realities kept pace with his holiness'. He ignored the confessional-box; offered his priests a sensible and not over-optimistic talk, beginning with the Paternoster, which they might give to penitents set upon vengeance; he worked hard at the erection of fraternities to make peace between members and among outsiders like Borromeo's. He was a Genoese, and had, as it were, read his Raggio.[37]

So those who worked under Borromeo's influence did not necessarily share his relative coolness, as I judge, towards the moral tradition. But there was a tension in his legacy which inspired his first biographer, Agostino Valier, bishop of Verona, to recommend a 'cautious imitation' of the future saint to his cousin and successor Federico. Valier's view was that holiness needed to be subordinate to charity, and zeal to patience; zeal might indeed be a disguise for the sin of anger, and cause far more trouble with the laity, the parish priests and the civil authorities

[36] Molinari, *Il Cardinale Paolo Burali*, pp. 37–8, 285–6, 335–44; Daniele Montanari, 'L'immagine del parroco nella riforma cattolica', *Archivo storico per le province parmensi*, 4th series, 30 (1978), pp. 93–105.

[37] F. Casta, *Evêques et curés corses dans la tradition pastorale du Concile de Trente* (Ajaccio, 1965), pp. 110, 135–40, and note p. 141 on the *impositio manus* after confession; Marc Venard, 'The Influence of Carlo Borromeo on the Church of France', in Headley and Tomaro, *San Carlo Borromeo*, p. 210 n. 8. On feud in Corsica, F. Braudel, *The Mediterranean and the Mediterranean World in the Age of Philip II* (2 vols., London, 1975), I, p. 36; Stephen Wilson, *Feuding, Conflict and Banditry in 19th Century Corsica* (Cambridge, 1988).

than it was worth.[38] Valier did not discuss peacemaking; but there were contemporaries of Borromeo for whom it was a central matter, and they may be said to have constituted a sort of official opposition to the Borromean mode. Since Paolo Prodi published his classic biography in the climate of the second Vatican Council, Gabriele Paleotti, archbishop of Bologna from 1565 to 1595, has figured, properly, as a different sort of model bishop from the one we are used to. A critical friend of Borromeo, his reservations perhaps arose from his earlier history as a law professor in Bologna: they included a sympathy with 'decent human custom' and a distaste for legislation, compulsion and new administrative structures. Paleotti erected in Bologna his own Congregazione della Concordia, staffed by Dominicans, as a forum for the extra-legal pacification of disputes. This was a much grander effort than Borromeo's, and clearly over-ambitious; although Paleotti made efforts not to tread on the corns of the legal profession, he was not successful, and his invention did not last. But it is not the only sign of his priorities. On his visitations, to general astonishment, he pursued *inconfessi* for *inimicizia* into their hideouts in the mountains and persuaded them, we are told, to peace and the sacraments. He expounded the sacraments as social institutions in the moral tradition, and his exposition of confession was constructed around the deadly sins, not the Commandments; at Trent, where he had worked hard, he had been in favour of communion in both kinds, though not of other Lutheran innovations. Dermot Fenlon has criticised him for obstructing the campaign of the papacy as a civil power against banditry, for which Gregory XIII and especially Sixtus V were famous. The answer to that, I think, as we can discover from Raggio, is that banditry and the moral tradition were hard to separate. Both entailed the

---

[38] *De cauta imitatione sanctorum episcoporum* (1595; printed in *Spicilegium Romanum*, VIII (Rome, 1842), pp. 89–116), pp. 93, 100, 102, 105–6, 108, 111.

resolution of offences by peace and family composition, not by the criminal law; sanctuary, which Paleotti defended against the papal administration, was a standard recourse for *banditi* and provided time for settlements.[39]

Paleotti may have been a little high-flown, a bit too theoretical, too much the professor for his own good or that of his diocese. With Domenico Bollani, bishop of Brescia, we have someone very down to earth. He was not a saint or a hero, and Borromeo acidly rebuked him for leaving Brescia during the plague. He was a civil servant and ex-diplomat of the Venetian Republic, and was *podestà* of Brescia, and a layman, at the time he was appointed bishop. His biographer says that arbitration and pacification were 'the keynote of Bollani's pastoral image'. During the Jubilee of 1575 he managed a public reconciliation between two leading families in Brescia, before the high altar of his cathedral; he was a successful joint-arbitrator of a long-standing civil dispute between Brescia and Cremona. The claim is pretty well borne out by an account of his episcopal activities. He had, we are told, a holistic view of church and state which came from his Venetian background and career; on his visitations he took his time, and talked as much to the *sindaci* and others of the commune as to the priest and churchwardens (so did Borromeo, but he was in more of a hurry). In his personal visitations (1565–7) we find detailed narratives of the histories of *inconfessi* for *inimicizia* or otherwise; from his successors we get little more than the publication of names and interdicts, or an equally unsatisfactory *omnia bene*. He

---

[39] Paolo Prodi, *Il Cardinale Gabriele Paleotti* (2 vols., Rome 1959–67), I, pp. 139–40 (communion), II, p. 33 (*paci*), pp. 47–8 (Borromeo), 127–8 (sacraments), 189ff (*Cong. Della Concordia*); Turchini, '"A beneficio pubblico . . ."', p. 237; M. Turrini, *La coscienza e le leggi* (Bologna, 1991), pp. 233ff (deadly sins); Dermot Fenlon, review of Prodi in *Scottish Journal of Theology*, 44 (1991), p. 124, cf. Prodi, *Paleotti*, II, pp. 373ff, 384; Raggio, *Faide e parentele*, chaps. 1 and 8. A bandit (*bandito*) is a man who has been outlawed for a criminal offence, often done in retaliation, by a court whose authority he has not recognised.

was no Paleotti, but he knew what he was doing. He said things about Borromeo which went rather beyond the 'cautious imitation' of Valier: absurd zealotry, piles of laws, no idea of the practicable, priest and people driven to desperation, the things that mattered not done. On the positive side, I think he was the only Italian bishop of the time to require his parish priests to possess a copy of William Durandus's liturgical exposition of the moral tradition, the *Rationale divinorum officiorum*.[40]

The Italian episcopate of the Counter-Reformation left behind it, if not exactly two models, two versions of the same model. The stricter, which became identified with Carlo Borromeo, was most influential in France from some time later; the laxer, in spite of Paleotti's lack of obvious success, in Italy. In the peninsula, the wet outlasted the dry. We are told on various hands that 'Tridentine' reform in Italy had more or less collapsed by about 1630. The tight parochial model decayed and fragmented through the seventeenth and eighteenth centuries in the face of a *revanche* of religious orders and fraternities. Fraternities drifted back to the free-standing guildhalls and oratories which Borromeo had sharply attacked; they boomed, not least the *casacce* of Genoa and Liguria, until the arrival of the French at the end of the eighteenth century. Football on Sunday afternoons, as it would, survived the competition of catechism.[41] Much of this story is unwritten; but

---

[40] C. Cairns, *Domenico Bollani* (Nieuwkoop, 1976), pp. 155–6, 177, 248–9; Daniele Montanari, *Disciplinamento in terra veneta* (Bologna, 1987), pp. 46–7 (on Borromeo, also quoted by Giuseppe Alberigo in Headley and Tomaro, *San Carlo Borromeo*, p. 255 and n), 62–4, 125 (Durandus), 184ff; G. Gamba and D. Montanari, in C. Nubola and A. Turchini (eds.), *Visite pastorali ed elaborazione dei dati* (Bologna, 1993), pp. 169–247, esp. pp. 196–203.

[41] Eric Cochrane, ed. Julius Kirshner, *Italy, 1530–1630* (London, 1988), pp. 199–202 (moderate); Mario Rosa, 'Organizzazione ecclesiastica e vita religiosa in Lombardia . . .', in *Problemi di storia religiosa lombarda* (Como, 1972), which I cite via Danilo Zardin, *Confraternite e vita di pietà . . . La pieve di Parabiago-Legnano* (Milan, 1981), pp. 34, 56; *ibid.*, pp. 54, 58, 245ff; E. Grendi, 'Le confraternite come fenomeno associativo e religioso', in C. Russo (ed.), *Società, chiesa e vita religiosa nell 'Ancien Regime'*

we can see something of what was happening from the story of the parish in seventeenth-century Piedmont sketched by Angelo Torre. Here we find, in the doings of an otherwise unmemorable set of successors to the militaristic Broglia, a sort of creative compromise emerging between the different trends in the Italian episcopate, and between them and the population. This *pace*, so to call it, entailed a multiplication of new parishes, which was always popular with communities and for which there was plenty of room; and the recognition of the parish as a 'composite entity' which was Bollani's advantage over Borromeo. Side-chapels and oratories were auctioned off to families, fraternities and neighbourhoods; sweetened with a tax-break, the demand contentedly mopped up the supply, and everybody was happy except the shade of San Carlo. I have the impression that these arrangements were made rather widely, and dissolved some of the tensions created in the age of high episcopalism. Some of them, from our point of view, may look ambiguous. In Liguria the pressure for new parishes might come from single *parentele* who did not want to come face to face with their rivals at the rites and festivals of the larger *pieve*. It is hard to say whether in such cases bishops were encouraging people to opt out of the moral tradition, or prudently safeguarding it from excessive strain.[42]

In tradition, as embodied by Alessandro Manzoni in *I Promessi Sposi*, but probably in fact, the outstanding episcopal personality of the age was Federico Borromeo, Carlo's cultivated younger cousin and successor in the see of Milan for thirty years or more (1595–1631). He has been variously judged. As presented by Paolo Prodi – and by myself following him – his work was a

---

(Naples, 1976), pp. 115–86; Zardin, *Riforma cattolica e resistenze nobiliari*, pp. 34–53 (football (*pallone*) versus catechism).

[42] Angelo Torre, 'Politics Cloaked in Worship: State, Church and Local Power in Piedmont, 1570–1770', *Past and Present*, no. 134 (1992), pp. 42–92; Raggio, *Faide e parentele*, pp. 227–60.

routinised version of his cousin's, propping up a vacuous concept of hierarchy in an age of economic and political disaster for his people. Anthony Wright has rejected the judgement, and seen little difference between the two apart from Federico's more genial way of life. Neither line seems satisfactory. Despite his terrified veneration for Carlo, the strongest personal influences on his adult career came from the critical side: from Valier, who addressed his critique of Carlo to him personally; from Paleotti; and from the alternative saint-figure of Philip Neri, whose cult of the Piovano Arlotto ought to be remembered at this point. Pamela Jones contrasts his humanistic 'optimism' with the Augustinian pessimism of Carlo: this is to paint with a broad brush, but accurately enough.[43]

In 1608 Federico Borromeo conducted a visitation in and around Lecco on Lake Como, as it happens the scene of the opening of the *Promessi Sposi*. He suspended a man from communion for not accepting a decent *pace* offered by the killer of his brother. He preached, at Lecco and probably elsewhere, two sermons on peace and enmity which are preserved in the visitation record. One picked up a common theme about pursuers of *inimicizia* doing more harm to themselves than to their enemies; *inimicizia* was rude, rustic and uncivilised. The other revived the traditionalist notion, expounded by William Durandus, of the Incarnation as a universal *pace*. There does not seem to be a precedent for it in Carlo's homilies; and I should think there were few precedents at all for his addition to the forms of Christian peace of the peace

---

[43] *The Betrothed*, chaps. 22–8 – the problem which provides the story is solved jointly by Federico and a bandit; P. Prodi, 'Nel iv° centinaio di Federico Borromeo: note biografiche e bibliografiche', *Convivium* (Bologna), 33 (1965), pp. 337–59; my own 'Postscript' to Evennett, *Spirit of the Counter-Reformation*, p. 138; Wright, 'Post-Tridentine Reform', pp. 211ff; L. Ponnelle and L. Bordet, *Saint Philip Neri and the Roman Society of his Time* (London, 1932; repr. 1979), pp. 56–62 (Piovano Arlotto), 493–9; Pamela Jones, *Federico Borromeo and the Ambrosiana* (Cambridge and New York, 1993), chap. 1 and *passim*.

to be received from communion with the natural world, which the lucky people of Lecco might breathe in from their valleys, their woods and their shining lake. The two conceptions, of the Incarnation and the Creation, ran together in Federico's sensitive mind: he had no doubt that peace was more than a matter of civility.[44]

Under the more relaxed episcopal regime which occupied the century or so between the death of Federico Borromeo and the coming of the Enlightenment, one may imagine many parish priests continuing to manage the machinery of annual confession and communion in the spirit of the moral tradition. But if we are looking for the most visible channel of the tradition in the age of the baroque we shall need to return to a topic we may have forgotten: to the country missions which had been invented by Landini and the Jesuits in the middle of the sixteenth century. In the following decades we can find Jesuits, who would have preferred a more impressive career in the Indies, nevertheless working patiently at peacemaking in out-of-the-way places in the papal state, while elsewhere they hunted heresy or taught catechism or, as in the Milanese and perhaps the Veneto, were not allowed to missionise at all. During the seventeenth century they got it down to a system: a week's mission, preaching of pardon on Friday, followed by grand reconciliation, penitential procession on Saturday, communion on Sunday; much drama, flagellation, bare feet, crowns of thorns. This machine invites many of the objections suggested by a strict application of the *status animarum* to Easter communion. Despite or because of the charisma of many of the missioners, it seems rather likely that the gimmicks

---

[44] C. Marcora (ed.), *La pieve di Lecco ai tempi di Federico Borromeo: degli atti della visita pastorale del 1608* (Lecco, 1979), pp. 28–9, 204, 622–4; cf. my own 'The Mass as a Social Institution', *Past and Present*, no. 100 (1983), p. 34. As well as Bollani's instruction (above p. 23), Nubola and Turchini, *Visite pastorali*, pp. 74ff, show that Durandus was in circulation in the region.

and arm-twisting which were needed to keep to the timetable often made for a superficial or indeed a contrary effect.[45]

Jesuit dominance in the field was challenged by others, notably by Vincent de Paul's Lazarists who, encouraged perhaps for political reasons by Pope Barberini, began operations around Rome about 1640 and spread thereafter through much of north-west Italy. Their mission was a great success, and its success came largely from the seriousness with which they cultivated the moral tradition.[46] At least for the male half of the population, re-conciliation was the principal object of their doings. They worked in appropriate fields: the papal state, Genoa and its territories including Corsica, Piedmont. In all of them the model described by Raggio applied: if counter-reformation *disciplina* or state formation had superseded it elsewhere in Italy, it had not done so there. The Lazarists confronted the ethics of feud. Probably what they said was much the same as what the Jesuits said: forgiveness of trespasses, the consequences of not forgiving, exclusion from communion for a start. They said it more simply and perhaps more quietly, avoiding hell-fire. They required the standard audible expressions and visible acts of reconciliation, from con-gregations where men, armed to the teeth in Corsica, might think their own thoughts or walk out in disgust. But they had, or may have borrowed from the Jesuits, the useful idea of asking first for the kissing of a crucifix, which evidently stood to the formal acts of reconciliation as kissing the *pax* at mass did to the embracing of enemies. In two respects their practice seems to have surpassed their Jesuit model in working with the grain of real life. This was certainly true in respect of time. They stayed in parishes a month

---

[45] Prosperi, 'Il missionario', pp. 211–18; *idem, Tribunali della coscienza*, pp. 597–8, 642–9; Louis Châtellier, *La religion des pauvres* (Paris, 1993), pp. 64, 205, 209; Gentilcore, ' "Adapt Yourselves . . ." ', pp. 280–1.

[46] P. Coste, *The Life and Labours of St Vincent de Paul* (3 vols., London, 1934–5), III, pp. 47–64; Gentilcore, ' "Adapt Yourselves . . ." ', pp. 273, 283.

or more; worked at 'loosening knots' until parties at enmity on account of a murder, an insult or a crashed marriage were willing to come and make a proper *pace* in church; waited for propitious days like Corpus Christi. Sometimes they could not stay long enough: at Cherasco in Piedmont in 1658, forty days could not bring the parties to agree, and the missioners left a town unreconciled. I think they probably also differed from the Jesuits in another respect. They are known, as Vincent's rule required, for cultivating relations with parish priests and not, as some Jesuits may have done, descending like gods from a machine. They are less known for cultivating relations with notaries. The thing that makes me believe that their missions of peacemaking were more than a flash in the pan is that they always, so far as I can see, required that the reconciliations they promoted should be properly registered by a notary.[47] We hear of notaries spending a week writing out *paci* until their arms dropped off: overworked, but not I imagine underpaid. As Raggio has explained, the notary was the central personage in the moral tradition as practised in Italy; the missionaries had put their finger on the spot. I do not think we need to respond with scepticism to the achievements they claimed: we may believe that people were often waiting for a suitable occasion to lay down the burden of social hostility without dishonour. A mission might be just this kind of jubilee; it also had the advantage over annual communion that the spectre of law was not present to disturb the proceedings.

On that unexpectedly cheerful note I pass across the Alps, leaving the Italian scene for the French. My conclusion is that the relation between moral tradition and Counter-Reformation in

---

[47] Coste, *Vincent de Paul*, III, p. 64 (Cherasco), 50–3, 55, 58. I find only one case where a Jesuit mentions fetching a notary, and that was to a dying man (Prosperi, *Tribunali della coscienza*, p. 647); no doubt it was common enough, but it does not seem to have been part of the strategy. Cf. Origo, *San Bernardino*, p. 19, on Vincent Ferrer, who was a famous peacemaker and took a notary with him on his preaching tours.

Italy was mixed, but on the whole surprisingly positive. I express surprise, because it seems to me that there were intrinsic difficulties, both with the harder-edged sort of Tridentine episcopalism, and with the activist ethos of the Jesuits and their like. Peace-making had an old-fashioned, unstrenuous, earthbound, one might say populist air which did not instantly recommend it to improvers and reformers, whether humanistic *spirituali* or dyed-in-the-wool *zelanti*. It might be thought to concede too much to barbarous or unchristian *mores*. It was not favoured by the panic which ensued upon the thunderclap of the Reformation in the north; by the institution of the Roman Inquisition; by the conclusions of the Council of Trent; nor, all told, by the charismatic doings of Carlo Borromeo. The strenuous climate of the late sixteenth century was not its natural milieu. It is a tribute to the moral sensitivity or simple realism of many of those who laboured in that climate that it came out of the storm in a distinctly healthy condition. I guess that its survival, it may be its enhancement, was a weighty influence in securing the continued loyalty of Italians to their church.

France

'In the seventeenth century', said Evennett in his lectures, 'the torch [of the Counter-Reformation] was passed to France'.[1] Yes, more or less. As we follow our story into France, we need to bear in mind a number of things which will be likely to make it different from that of Italy. There are the French Protestants, cheek-by-jowl with Catholics from the massive desertion of the mid-sixteenth century until, and after, their intended extirpation by Louis XIV. There is the crown, which controls the French church, or at least the episcopate, from Henri IV onwards; it also has a virtual monopoly of law and government from way back. We cannot imagine the state of affairs in Raggio's Liguria obtaining as a stable condition anywhere in the kingdom of France.

It is an important difference. The moral tradition is not quite here the matter of life and death it may often seem to be in Italy. This has consequences in real life, and also in what has been written by historians. For historians of France the interesting question has not generally been about peace, but about 'community'. These are certainly connected notions, but they are not quite the same thing. The notion 'community' drifts towards an ideal type of collective togetherness which takes it above the level of actual human relations: I shall do my best to break it down. One more point about the historiography. Behind nearly all the work

---

[1] Evennett, *Spirit of the Counter-Reformation*, p. 18.

which will be germane to the subject in France, there looms as a great shadow the Giant Dechristianisation. What seem to be the grandeurs of the French church from the sixteenth century to the eighteenth lead into a time of fairly grandiose collapse, the features of which can be seen in the famous *Carte religieuse de la France rurale*. Two of our best historians, Marc Venard and Robin Briggs, have complained about the preoccupation, and surely with justice; I cannot claim that I have escaped the giant's shadow, though I have tried.[2]

I start by sketching the state of the moral tradition in France in the time of the wars of religion; and do so, as I say, by peeling off layers from the onion of community as it appears, in this crisis, from the Catholic side of the table. The classic depiction of it, as every schoolgirl knows, is Natalie Davis's 'The Rites of Violence'. Here we meet, in all its ungovernable force, the notion of holy togetherness which lay behind the Massacre of St Bartholomew and similar events: an Aztec togetherness which, as on a Corpus Christi festival or *Fête-Dieu*, demanded for the salvation of all the extermination of those who undid it by blasphemy, mockery or simple non-participation. I take her description as conclusive; and what she describes, as an exasperated version of 'the "community" as the vessel of a supernatural solidarity'.[3] Whether it is a version of the moral tradition may be disputed. If it is not, I do not think it can be because it entails murdering one's neighbours: the moral tradition is certainly

---

[2] G. Le Bras, *Etudes de sociologie religieuse* (2 vols., Paris, 1955–6), at p. 324, has the *Carte*; Marc Venard, 'L'Eglise d'Avignon au XVIe siècle' (Service de Reproduction de Thèses, Lille, 1980), p. 1923; Robin Briggs, *Communities of Belief: Cultural and Social Tensions in Early Modern France* (Oxford, 1989), p. 412.

[3] Natalie Z. Davis, 'The Rites of Violence: Religious Riot in 16th Century France', *Past and Present*, no. 59 (1973), pp. 53–91, and in her *Society and Culture in Sixteenth Century France* (London, 1975), pp. 152–87; cf. Denis Crouzet, *Les guerriers de Dieu* (2 vols., Seyssel, 1990), II, pp. 128, 287ff, 322 on the 'processions blanches'; Venard, 'L'Eglise d'Avignon', p. 1943.

compatible with the burning of witches. But it does need, as they say, unpacking.

When we unpack it, we come to the fraternity, and that much closer to the moral tradition, in that participation in a fraternity meant a willingness to settle disputes with one's brothers or sisters by peaceful and non-legal means. Wherever the forces of Catholicism got themselves together in France, from the 1560s to the 1590s, the fraternity appeared: very traditional fraternities like the Confréries du Saint-Esprit which in much of the south-east were virtually equivalent to the community in the local sense; new ones like the brotherhoods of Pénitents. These were a revival of the Italian flagellant fraternities of *disciplinati*, which took off in France when they were running into difficulties in Italy: they started in Avignon in the 1530s. They, or their more enthusiastic members, were committed to frequent communion, which in principle stood rather in the way of their sociable functions. But the principle may not have mattered much in the electric atmosphere of the late sixteenth century, and when the crisis was over the Pénitents gave up frequent communion anyway. Fraternities were spontaneous because they were voluntary and because they were not inspired by the bishops, who generally disliked them as divisive, anti-parochial, unmanageable; it is not so surprising that in Avignon there was a general panic that the pope, spiritual as well as temporal sovereign, was about to abolish them.[4]

---

[4] Jean Gutton, 'Confraternities, Curés and Communities in Rural Areas of the Diocese of Lyon under the Ancien Régime', in K. von Greyerz (ed.), *Religion and Society in Early Modern Europe* (London, 1984), pp. 202–11, and his other works there cited; Marc Venard, 'Les confréries de Pénitents au XVIe siècle', *Mémoires de l'Académie de Vaucluse*, 6th series, 1 (1967), pp. 55–79; my own 'Leagues and Associations in 16th Century French Catholicism', *Studies in Church History*, XXIII: *Voluntary Religion*, ed. W. J. Sheils and Diana Wood (Oxford, 1986), pp. 171–89; Venard, 'L'Eglise d'Avignon', p. 750. Weissman, *Ritual Brotherhood in Renaissance Florence*, p. 224.

Listen, by contrast, to Jean Bodin, whose private opinions are in dispute but who ended his public life in the Catholic League. Book III, chapter 7 of his *Six livres de la République* (1576) is a defence of fraternal institutions as embodiments of moral tradition and essential items in the commonwealth. 'Men, led by a sociable and companionable instinct, establish such communities and associations'; they are founded on friendship and goodwill, which need them in order to survive. 'To ask whether [they] are necessary to the commonwealth, is to ask whether the commonwealth can subsist without friendship, which even the world itself cannot do.' (Was he talking of sympathies in the universe?) The prime characteristic of such associations was that they settled disputes among members by arbitration, like the Swiss.[5]

Bodin's account of fraternity does not explicitly require unity of faith among participants, and hence evokes the fine discussion of the bedrock of the moral tradition to be found in Gregory Hanlon's book about the small Gascon town of Layrac. Hanlon is reacting to Natalie Davis by claiming that there is a peace-history as well as a war-history of French Christianity in the age of the wars of religion; I do not, myself, think that it makes any difference to the accuracy of Davis's description to agree that he must be right about this. In Layrac, as in much of southern France, where resemblances to Italy were strong, the moral tradition was carried by the *consuls* or elected local councillors and by the notaries, not by the priests. The town was divided between Protestants and Catholics, the Protestants at this time the more influential. The Protestant consistory worked very hard at the moral tradition, as it has been shown to do elsewhere in the

[5] From the abridged English translation by M. J. Tooley, *Six Books of the Commonwealth* (Oxford, n.d.), p. 105 and in general pp. 96–107; cf. my 'Leagues and Associations', pp. 186–7, and Gregory Hanlon, *Confession and Community in 17th Century France: Catholic and Protestant Co-Existence in Aquitaine* (Philadelphia, 1993), p. 185, on conflict settlement as the great effect of the Pénitents.

Midi: its main activity was to settle disputes and hostilities among members of the congregation, to twist the arms of those bent on litigation in order, I take it, to prepare them for communion as well as to compete with, or show up, the Catholics. It was behaving, one may say, like the rectors of a model fraternity.[6]

For the 'community' as a whole, there was pressure from the leaders of both sides to use the institutions of peace and sociability to accommodate relations between believers of the two faiths for the 'bien de la république'. Arrangements were made about elections to the consulate, which were followed by interconfessional feasting: Protestants danced at Carnival, to the irritation of their ministers; mixed marriage and godparenthood kept relations going. We are not simply dealing with prudent co-existence, but with something inevitably felt to be Christian – 'bonne amytié . . . bonne paix'. Formal agreements to this effect were rather common in the south, often in the 1590s, it is true, in the general state of exhaustion produced at the end of the wars. But not all of them date from this time. In 1568, from Saint-Laurent-des-Arbres, north of Avignon, we have a notarial act affirming that the population, on the advice of its *baille* and consuls, has resolved 'to make a good and holy confederation between all the people, to swear peace and friendship to each other, and to help each other in full brotherhood (*en toute fraternité*), nothing being more wished by the common body of the said council than to live together as brothers in concord and friendship'. Such agreements, as Venard says, were as vulnerable as any other kind of peace; in Layrac concord survived until about 1620, when an aggressive priest and a change in the balance of numbers began to upset it.[7]

---

[6] Hanlon, *Confession and Community, passim*, esp. pp. 73–90; B. Vogler and J. Estèbe, 'La genèse d'une société protestante; étude comparée de quelques registres consistoriaux languedociens et palatins vers 1600', *Annales*, 31 (1976), pp. 365–6, 378–9.

[7] Hanlon, *Confession and Community*, pp. 39–73, 91–116; Venard, 'L'Eglise d'Avignon', pp. 805–8, 1558–9.

My more conventional illustration comes from Lorraine, so cannot count as French; but it is the best I can do. Pierre Fourier was the curate of Mattaincourt, an artisan settlement south of Nancy, for some thirty years from 1597. He was well educated, notably in Thomist theology and both laws, and well connected, though his roots were local and demotic. He was a prudent sceptic about witchcraft, and an early health-bore; he had a fund of ideas about charity, *raison d'état* and the education of girls. He was also in the position, perhaps unknown in the kingdom of France, of possessing the right of high and low justice in his parish: this, his legal training, and observation of a charitable or business-minded *avocat* rapidly settling disputes on market-day in the neighbouring town of Mirecourt, persuaded him to use his authority for the systematic promotion of arbitration. He sat in front of his house with a pair of parish worthies chosen annually on the *Fête-Dieu* to hear and mediate. No doubt there was some arm-twisting, but altogether Fourier seems to have been a success with the population and died in the odour of sanctity as a model priest. Towards the end of his life he planned a society of nobles and lawyers to settle cases on the spot and free of charge throughout the duchy. Since he was aware of things Italian, influence from Paleotti or Borromeo may be possible; like theirs, Fourier's idea came to nothing, swept away when the Thirty Years War fell upon Lorraine in 1636.[8]

Lorrainer as he was, Fourier takes us into that star-studded period of French Catholicism chronicled by Henri Bremond, which covers the first half of the seventeenth century. Some of these stars were rather high-flying for my parochial purposes, but I start with one of them, François de Sales. From 1602 to 1622

---

[8] René Taveneaux, 'La pensée et l'œuvre sociales de St Pierre Fourier', in *Lyon et l'Europe: Mélanges d'histoire offerts à Richard Gascon* (2 vols., Lyon, 1980), II, pp. 267–78; Donald Attwater, *Penguin Dictionary of Saints* (London, 1965), p. 280.

bishop in theory of Geneva and in fact of an alpine diocese based on Annecy, de Sales was the most respected francophone bishop of his time. He was no more a Frenchman than Fourier because his background and his diocese were in the Duchy of Savoy, but much of his work was done in Paris and his principal contacts were French. I have been tempted to think of him as an extension of the moral-tradition episcopate of contemporary Italy, or of Torre's Piedmontese, with whom he shared a prince. But it looks as if the temptation ought to be resisted. He had been a student in Paris at the height of the wars of religion, and his first sermon was about them: he invited his hearers to be of one mind, since if there was peace on earth to men of good will, war was a punishment for men of bad will. This may remind us of Federico Borromeo, but the resemblance must be accidental, because the relation between the two was distant, and François's Italian not good.[9]

The image returns at the beginning of his *Advice to Confessors* of 1603–4: your works, he tells them, are the channels through which 'peace flows from heaven to earth upon men of good will'. Hence the priest was to be patient with the 'rusticity, feebleness and dilatoriness' of the peasantry. De Sales respected Carlo Borromeo, though he did not admire his learning; but he was tepid about the confessional-box, and retained the *impositio manus* at absolution. On one occasion we find him, like Philip Neri, embracing a (male) penitent who had particularly pleased him by his candour. In his account of sins he kept a careful balance between the sins of hostility and the sins of concupiscence; he was known to detest disputes among Catholics, and made a couple of practical gestures for pacifying relations between priests and population. Where the parishioner did not wish to confess and

[9] *Œuvres de St François de Sales* (27 vols., Annecy, 1892–1964), VII, p. 22 (1593), also IX, p. 286 (1620), XVII, pp. 156–7 (to Federico Borromeo); P. Broutin, *La réforme pastorale en France au XVIIe siècle* (2 vols., Tournai, 1956), I, pp. 89ff.

communicate with him, the *curé* was to give him permission to go elsewhere without asking questions; no *curé* was to start a lawsuit with his parishioners without getting permission from his superiors, who would do their best to arbitrate the dispute.[10]

These *Advertissements* give François de Sales an honourable place in the moral tradition, but do not seem to have had much impact on the French church; though his name was much used, his influence as a bishop was limited. He had, of course, a huge audience as the author of the *Introduction à la vie dévote*, but that was something else. Women, for whom the *Introduction* was written, might in the common view upset peace by slander, gossip or malefice; they could rarely bring it about. François quotes St Louis quite a lot in the book, but does not mention him sitting under the tree at Vincennes settling disputes.[11] Hence the state of the moral tradition in early seventeenth-century France, whatever it will turn out to be, will probably owe less to de Sales than to the regime of benign neglect under which the French episcopal order operated in the days of Cardinal Richelieu. There *were* active bishops, like the Borromean François de Sourdis of Bordeaux, who arrived in Paris in 1625 with a reputation of sanctity for having held a provincial council. But altogether the impression is of *laissez-faire*. Nothing doing in the see of Paris under the house of Gondi, nor in Reims under the house of Guise; chaos, possibly, in the huge archdiocese of Chartres, running from the Seine to beyond the Loire and effectively governed by its archdeacons.

---

[10] *Œuvres de St François de Sales*, XXIII, pp. 279–97, 307, 309, 396, 397. It appears that at some point de Sales required the confessions of women to be heard in confessionals (Broutin, *Réforme pastorale en France*, I, pp. 89ff, as of Synod of 1617; against this, *Œuvres de St François de Sales*, XXIII, p. 395); on Borromeo's learning, M. Bernos (below, n. 20), p. 192; Montanari, 'L'immagine del parroco nella riforma cattolica', p. 110 (disputes).

[11] Philip T. Hoffman, *Church and Community in the Diocese of Lyon* (New Haven and London, 1984), p. 80, for an example of influence; *Introduction to the Devout Life*, ed. A. Ross, 2nd edn (London, 1943), especially part III.

No lack of visitations here; but visitations designed as a holiday tour for the archdeacon, a series of gourmet dinners with the priests at the parishes' expense. The priests, who were of an independent turn of mind, exchanged grainy repartee with the visitor and the parishioners; it seems they drank and smoked with their friends during long evenings at the inns, and womanised a good deal.[12]

There is, from our point of view, a lot to be said for episcopal *laissez-faire*. It left the people of Provence to get on with their multicoloured fraternities of Pénitents, or *gazettes*, to use the name they had borrowed from Liguria; and if, as Maurice Agulhon supposes, in these easier times their original combination of devotion and sociability was resolving itself in favour of the second, this was probably in the nature of the institution and no bad thing for the moral tradition. The Bretons were left to worry about their dead, the Burgundians about their wine.[13] *Laissez-faire* may also account for the lack of evidence for parochial peace-making in the visitations of the period, though there is some in the diocese of Paris: the *status animarum* was a very rare bird, and priests, it appears, cultivated their relations with the parish by simply not telling visitors about non-communicants, as villagers gratified the *curé* by not telling about his flirtations. I quote the great Gabriel Le Bras, who had more right to know than anybody:

[12] On Richelieu and the church: Joseph Bergin, *The Rise of Richelieu* (New Haven and London, 1991), chap. 3; *idem*, *The Making of the French Episcopate, 1589–1661* (New Haven and London, 1996), pp. 448–93. Bergin says (p. 448) that Richelieu was 'committed ... to improving the condition of the French church', so my description may be unfair. *Ibid.*, pp. 440–2 (Reims); otherwise P. Blet, *Le clergé de France et la monarchie* (2 vols., Rome, 1959), I, p. 268–9; J. Ferté, *La vie religieuse dans les campagnes parisiennes, 1622–1695* (Paris, 1962), pp. 19ff; R. Sauzet, *Les visites pastorales dans le diocèse de Chartres dans la première moitié du XVIIe siècle* (Rome, 1975), pp. 85, 96, 135ff, 237ff.

[13] Maurice Agulhon, *Pénitents et francs-maçons de l'ancienne Provence* (Paris, 1968), pp. 86–123; Alain Croix, *La Bretagne aux XVIe–XVIIe siècles: la vie, la mort, la foi* (Paris, 1981), pp. 943–1154, 1241–2; Mack Holt, 'Wine, Community and Reformation in 16th Century Burgundy', *Past and Present*, no. 138 (1993), pp. 58–93.

We know that under the *Ancien Régime*, denunciations by name of absentees from the Easter sacraments, so full of risks for the personal tranquillity [of the clergy], did not occur in many parishes, except where there were scandals or quarrels, or to prevent absenteeism from becoming a habit (*interrompre la prescription*) . . . We also know that the clergy found the publishing of censures distasteful. They hesitated, without any doubt, to denounce peaceful late-comers (*les retardataires paisibles*) [on whom compare François de Sales, above].[14]

The obscurity of the period is lightened by the emergence of rural missionising as it came in from Italy, perhaps via the Capuchins who were doing a lot of it over the frontier in Savoy and Catholic Switzerland. We have seen what an impact Vincent de Paul's Lazarists had when imported into Italy, and though the immediate domestic achievement of this collaborator and successor of Richelieu may seem less dramatic, his institution of the Priests of the Mission in 1625 is a date to remember in the story of the moral tradition in France. Traditionally one has seen Vincent de Paul as the promoter of a very powerful but different notion of charity: charity as a work, and notably a work of assistance to the poor. Important, pathfinding, and surely necessary as this was, it has put rather into the shade his commitment to the older mode of charity. In the objects of the Priests of the Mission reconciling actually comes higher than setting up the Confraternities of Charity which were to pursue the works of charity; this may reflect a division of labour between his male and female followers. He very firmly told one of his priests, who thought it none of his business, that he was to work at reconciliation, and to hold frequent meetings with 'two devout, pacific and intelligent'

---

[14] Ferté, *Vie religieuse*, pp. 318, 320–1; Sauzet, *Visites pastorales*, pp. 108, 227, 239; Briggs, *Communities of Belief*, pp. 262–6; Le Bras, *Etudes de sociologie religieuse*, I, pp. 214–15. Venard, 'The Influence of Carlo Borromeo', pp. 216ff, says that the *status animarum* did not take off in France.

parishioners to attend to it. The work of his missioners was rather interrupted by Richelieu's wars and consequent tax crises, but by the 1640s we find them at work in various parts of the country, as around Saint-Malô in Brittany, where they extended the policy of gradualism visible in Italy by settling as semi-permanent residents and taking a very long-term view of their activity, in reconciliation and otherwise.[15]

Such signs of the vitality of the moral tradition in France must, as we come up to the majority of Louis XIV, be balanced against signs that a climate was emerging in the French church which might not be very favourable to it. The third of the trinity of its seventeenth-century founding fathers, Pierre de Bérulle, had a formidably vertical view of religion which mixed the hierarchical and the mystical in a synthesis without much room for earthbound activities like peacemaking. Bérulle disapproved of the Priests of the Mission and had tried to dissuade Rome from authorising them.[16] Through his creation of the French Oratory and otherwise he was a long-term influence to set against that of Vincent de Paul. Then there was the passage, gradual and patchy as it was, towards the adoption of a Tridentine regime in the dioceses. We can get some idea of what this meant from the archdiocese of Lyon. In 1600 the parochial scene here was a benevolent-looking muddle of dancing and godparenting *curés, consuls*, brotherhoods of the Holy Spirit and three-day communal beanfeasts at Whitsun. Half a century later something had changed, but I am not sure how much. Vincent de Paul himself had appeared as a young and earnest reformer in 1617, but had retired to Paris. Before 1630 the main episcopal figure was a

---

[15] Jean Delumeau, 'Missions de l'intérieur au XVIIe siècle', in *Un chemin d'histoire* (Paris, 1981), pp. 181–5; Coste, *Vincent de Paul*, I, p. 540, III, pp. 22–46; Châtellier, *La religion des pauvres*, pp. 71–8.

[16] On Bérulle I have followed P. Cochois, *Bérulle et l'école française* (Paris, 1963); Coste, *Vincent de Paul*, I, p. 157.

mild admirer of François de Sales, often absent in Rome. Things began to happen then with the arrival of the devout pressure-group, the Compagnie du Saint-Sacrement, which networked among priests and royal officials to put down parish feasts, festive groups and banquets; it campaigned for the outward redirection of charity and put up schools. A priesthood with a Tridentine ethos would seep in with the establishment of seminaries around 1650, losing, we are told, its ties with the machinery of rural sociability. This seems plausible, if a little overdone: I notice, among regulations of an anti-social tendency, a prohibition of 'profane pacts and contracts' in church, which appears to exclude the ceremonies of notarised reconciliation familiar in neighbouring Italy, whose customs had a good deal in common with those of the region.[17]

Perhaps I may use my favourite test, the installation of the confessional-box, to give some kind of chronology to the emergence of this unwelcoming atmosphere. There were church councils from the period of the League which recommended or required it; but these were abortive efforts. One of the councils was held in Toulouse in 1590, and visitations from thirty years later show that the box was not a requisite then, any more than it was for François de Sales. Much concern about fonts and tabernacles; nothing about confessionals. According to Venard, the box only appeared on the borders of Italy, penetrating 'as it were by contagion', or where there was a very active bishop. In Normandy the first statutes requiring it date from 1618 in Rouen and 1644 in Evreux, and from statutes to installation there will have been a gap of indeterminate length: there were still 'often' no confessionals in the archdiocese of Rouen in 1700.

---

[17] Hoffman, *Church and Community in the Diocese of Lyon*, chaps. 2 and 3, p. 85 (contracts); Bergin, *Making of the French Episcopate*, p. 664, and index *s. v.* Marquemont, Denis Simon de.

It looks as if they were far from normal furniture before say 1660.[18]

I have probably said enough already about the consequences of the confessional-box in precipitating the disappearance of the laying-on of the hand, the visible sign of the sacrament of penance as a vehicle of the moral tradition. The coming of the box must also relate to the decline of the rite of public confession, which was well established in French practice at least to the end of the sixteenth century. It was a collective, parochial affair performed, in the vernacular, usually on Maundy Thursday or on Easter Sunday before communion. It was held by the learned to forgive venial sins, while mortal sins required private confession; in the admonition of the *curé* and the text of the confession the sins of mutual hatred were nearly always treated as the most import-ant. There were those in the seventeenth century who defended it as the expression of a 'public conscience' which protected the population as a whole from punishment for the sins of impenitent members; but the general tone of official comment and regulation was extremely hostile. I take it to express a conviction among spiritual authorities of all shades of opinion that the purpose of confession was the individual's reconciliation to God alone, and a backlash against the favour shown to the collective rite by Protestants. The campaign achieved its object as local liturgies were superseded by the Roman rite.[19]

[18] G. Baccrabère, 'La pratique religieuse dans le diocèse de Toulouse aux XVI–XVIIe siècles', *Annales du Midi*, 74 (1962), pp. 287, 362; Venard, 'The Influence of Carlo Borromeo', pp. 219–20; M. Join-Lambert, 'La pratique religieuse dans le diocèse de Rouen sous Louis XIV', *Annales de Normandie*, 3 (1953), p. 273. Cf. my 'Social History of Confession', pp. 29–33.

[19] 'Social History of Confession', pp. 22–4, quoting Johannes Gropper; Nicole Lemaître, 'Pratique et signification de la confession communautaire dans les paroisses au XVIe siècle', in Groupe de la Bussière, *Pratiques de la Confession* (Paris, 1983), pp. 139–64. Scattered references to the campaign against it, which might be multiplied, are in Hoffman, *Church and Community in the Diocese of Lyon*, pp. 71, 84; Hanlon,

What had hitherto been a sort of continental drift became a fairly intense pressure during the first thirty years of the reign of Louis XIV. If there was, in France, a period of critical conflict between moral tradition and Counter-Reformation, it is here that we must place it. Two things set it off: one to do with the church, and one to do with the state. In the church, the important event was the emergence of a new model to take the place of François de Sales; he was called 'St Charles', a title concealing Carlo Borromeo who had been canonised in 1610, or a version of him from which the complications had been removed. He entered the scene with a bang in 1643 with the publication of a version of his *Acta* and, more explosively, of Antoine Arnauld's *De la fréquente communion*. Arnauld held up for admiration the Borromean practice of deferring absolution to those whose repentance had not been tried by time, and defended the abstention from communion of the laity influenced by it. He held up for imitation the work and person of Borromeo as a whole, or at least the simplified model of it which appeared in the public record. In comparing him with de Sales, he admitted that Borromeo was a much stiffer model. This, he said, was because de Sales was dealing with a diocese full of Protestants where 'softly, softly' was the word, which it was not in the established Catholic dioceses of France.[20]

Arnauld's book was, of course, a sortie in the grand battle among the devout and the clergy between the Jesuit and the Jansenist ways. I do not see that battle as impinging very sharply on our subject. The Jesuit practice of the moral tradition did not extend beyond their rural missions, or influence their position in

---

Confession and Community, p. 155; Châtellier, *La religion des pauvres*, p. 210. It is not clear that all these cases are about a collective rite, rather than about *ad hoc* assemblies by parish priests.

[20] Antoine Arnauld, *De la fréquente communion*, 7th edn (Paris, 1683), esp. pp. 5–80 and chap. 44; M. Bernos, 'Saint Charles Borromée [et] le clergé français' in *Pratiques de la Confession*, pp. 185–200, at p. 195.

the dispute, which was about the sacramental behaviour of the devout; they were faithful to Ignatius's devotional view of the sacraments. Jansenist theology was probably unsympathetic to the contractual aspect of the moral tradition, and to the suggestion it carried that universal salvation was on the cards. But their practice might have supported it if the pacification of enmities had had a reasonable showing among the reasons why absolution might be deferred. I see no sign that it did. Robin Briggs, analysing the sort of sins envisaged, sees the weight of Jansenist concern falling on 'economic' sins and sexual/marital sins. Economic sins included usury and various sorts of greed and oppression practised by the rich on the poor: they involved restitution and were certainly social sins, sins against charity. But Briggs sees their emphasis on them, however laudable, as unrealistic and out of touch and, except in the case of the occasional strict-Jansenist bishop, as not having much connection with pastoral practice. Rightly or wrongly they claimed 'St Charles' as their authority, and succeeded in making him more than a party figure: he was, as it were, recanonised by the French secular clergy in 1657, when they made his *Instructions for Confessors* a set book for priests. Thereafter his status as *the* model bishop and pastor was established: it may be that his recanonisation in France brought the book back into the limelight in Italy.[21]

Trimmed of its cutting edge against the state, the Borromean model proved very acceptable to a government anxious to impose obedience upon the population: bureaucracy called to bureaucracy across the Alps. It seems to be a mistake to suppose that

---

[21] Briggs, *Communities of Belief*, pp. 314–23; cf. Jean Delumeau, *Le péché et la peur* (Paris, 1983), pp. 475–97; Bernos, 'Saint Charles Borromée', pp. 195–6. Delumeau's table, p. 477, shows no significant difference in the degree of preaching against envy and anger between San Bernardino and the French seventeenth century; but four-fifths of the seventeenth-century sermons are from missionaries. The *Instructions* were little used in Italy until the eighteenth century: Turrini, *La coscienza e le leggi*, pp. 115–16.

Louis XIV's episcopal bench was entirely staffed by Colberts and Le Telliers, but there were rather a lot of them, and perhaps they set the tone. The average bishop became, willy-nilly, what has been called an 'inspecteur administratif'; the visitation question-naire emerged, got longer and longer and was distributed in printed copies, like a tax form.[22] Simple conformity, if not the object of the bishops themselves, was surely the object of the state which appointed them. Two considerations hastened the push in this direction: the gathering persecution of French Protestants; and the conquest of new territories in the east. The first entailed a brutal intervention in the affairs of families, which rebounded upon Catholics, as in state legislation requiring instant baptism: I should have taken the particularity of this situation into account when arguing for an absolute conflict between Borromean Cath-olicism and family pieties.[23] Eastward expansion brought under the control of a French state-run church territories in Germany and the Netherlands which had a different tradition: I shall say something about this next time.[24]

'It is, no doubt,' says Marc Venard, 'precisely where Catholic reform penetrated most deeply . . . that "dechristianisation" . . . came earliest and has been most complete.'[25] Like Venard, we may not wish to give too much scope to the topic as such: our object must be to see whether we can account for his paradox by

[22] Briggs, *Communities of Belief*, pp. 208–34; immense questionnaires may be found in Join-Lambert, 'La pratique religieuse', and Le Bras, 'Etat religieux et moral du diocèse de Châlons au dernier siècle de l'Ancien Régime', in *Etudes de sociologie religieuse*, I, pp. 56–7.

[23] Elisabeth Labrousse, *Essai sur la Révocation de l'Edit de Nantes* (Geneva and Paris, 1985), pp. 157, 171–2, 201; my 'Counter-Reformation and the People of Catholic Europe', pp. 54–58, at p. 57 n. 22 (Edict of 1698); F. Charpin, *Pratique religieuse et formation d'une grande ville* (Paris, 1964), pp. 11–12, 19–20; Louis Pérouas, *La diocèse de La Rochelle de 1648 à 1724: sociologie et pastorale* (Paris, 1964), p. 327.

[24] See below, chap. 3, for Alsace; also Venard, 'The Influence of Carlo Borromeo', p. 223; A. Lottin, *Lille: citadelle de la Contreréforme?* (Westhoek, 1984), pp. 57, 313.

[25] Venard, 'L'Eglise d'Avignon', p. 1934.

a clash between Catholic reform and moral tradition. We can suspect it in the diocese of Châlons-sur-Marne in Champagne ('Cochons-sur-Marne' in the words of the nineteenth-century prophet Léon Bloy): forty years of the dedicated Borromean Félix Vialart and a century of bureaucracy made a territory of 'conformisme moutonnier' (ovine conformism) which greeted the Revolution with some enthusiasm and forms a black (actually, white) hole in the *Carte religieuse de la France rurale*.[26] We can see it in the diocese of Tarbes running up into the Pyrenees. Around 1600 this was a sleepy area where the previous century had added no new element except a hostility to Protestants; powerful fraternities of clergy and laity feasted and reconciled, as they needed to do. After an idle and concubinary bishop in the mid-century who was none the less, or therefore, a model of charity, it enjoyed the long episcopate of a *grand-réformateur*-cum-civil-servant who brought discipline to the flatlands but did not get far in the mountains. There, an entrenched communal Catholicism, *curés* taking the minutes and quarrelling fraternally with the *consuls*, guns and pilgrimages: a sort of anti-Montaillou. Result: in the flatlands, falling-away; in the mountains, Lourdes.[27]

Famously, there is Sennely-en-Sologne, the 'village immobile' in the Loire valley written up by its priest around 1700, and since by Gérard Bouchard. The people of Sennely were good Catholics: they hated Protestants, iconoclastic bishops and the gentry; they were charitable among themselves, keen on fraternities, pilgrimages, processions. But they abhorred confession, and fled from the confessional-box as from the mouth of hell: Sauvageon, the priest, had to listen to their grudging mumbles

[26] Le Bras, *Etudes de sociologie religieuse*, I, pp. 54–68, 324; Broutin, *Réforme pastorale en France*, I, pp. 226ff. It is proper to say that the situation is worse in the neighbouring dioceses of Troyes, Sens and (Bossuet's!) Meaux.

[27] J.-F. Soulet, *Traditions et réformes religieuses dans les Pyrénées centrales au XVIIe siècle* (Paris, 1974), pp. 47ff, 96ff, 199ff, 342–55, etc.: a classic study.

outside it. They were, he said, 'undisciplinable'. The shadow of the confessional-box fell between them and the church: their charity and solidarity would remain, but drift in other directions.[28]

From these instances we might make a powerful case for the fatal consequences of Catholic reform on the moral tradition. It would be far too simple, and for two reasons: that the distribution of episcopal bureaucracy or zeal is not identical with the distribution of blank patches on the *Carte religieuse*; and that the moral tradition did not die of drought even among the satellites of the Sun King. The diocese of La Rochelle, launched in 1648, covered a rural territory where dispute, generally through the law, was as endemic as anywhere else in the kingdom, and the moral tradition healthy: partly because of the effort put into it by the Reformed consistories in the past, and partly because its first bishop was a disciple of Vincent de Paul.[29] It then, in 1661, acquired a quasi-Jansenist in Henri de Laval, one of a trio of similarly minded bishops in the region known as the 'trois Henri'. For twenty years and more Laval saw, often from a distance, to the erection of an Augustinian regime of high churchmanship, high theology and high catechism designed, says his historian, to make of his diocese a 'community of faith': it proved to have little connection with any sort of community the actual population might wish to belong to. In the 1680s the diocese was virtually taken over by the state while it tried to dragoon the remaining Protestants into conversion. A recipe, one might think, for disaster; and indeed disaster is roughly what happened later on in most of the diocese. It did not happen in the northern third of it,

---

[28] Gérard Bouchard, *Le village immobile: Sennely-en-Sologne au XVIIIe siècle* (Paris, 1972), pp. 283–343. On confession, *ibid.*, pp. 291–2, 339; Delumeau, *Un chemin d'histoire*, pp. 173–80; Briggs, *Communities of Belief*, pp. 323–5.

[29] Pérouas, *Le diocèse de La Rochelle*, pp. 142, 161, 173–4, 176; the bishop, Jacques Raoul, *ibid.*, pp. 223–4; Coste, *Vincent de Paul*, III, p. 46; Delumeau, 'Missions de l'intérieur', p. 182; Bergin, *Making of the French Episcopate*, p. 688.

adjacent to the Vendée and continuing to share its views and habits. There is no sign of any pastoral preference given to the area, rather the reverse.[30]

After the death of Laval in 1693 the diocese experienced a return to the moral tradition during the episcopate of an otherwise unknown philo-Jesuit called Frézeau: no Paleotti, but perhaps another Bollani. Fraternal charity was his line. He arbitrated enmities, and set up ceremonies of reconciliation; told the peasants to keep off the law and settle before the *curé*; intervened between families at visitations.[31] He will not help us to identify the vitality of the moral tradition with the vitality of popular Catholicism; but he does point us in the direction of a large event in our story which, taken as a whole, will surely bear some such implication. For most of Louis XIV's reign the rural missions as conceived by Vincent de Paul seem to have suffered from the Borromeanism of the secular clergy and the harnessing of the religious orders to the oppressive objectives of the state. During the anti-Jansenist reaction of the king's last years, and at the beginning of the next reign, they came into their own. We have come to the time of Grignon de Montfort, whose early work was done under Frézeau's successor before he moved north into Brittany. Grignon was a star in the constellation of preachers who made the earlier eighteenth century a golden age for the rural mission and the feast of reconciliation its proper conclusion. In his popular canticles he set the moral tradition to music, in verse which expounded the plight of the cherisher of enmity who

> Ne dit jamais son *Pater*
> Qu'il ne se condamne a l'enfer.[32]
>
> (Every time he says his *Pater*
> Condemns himself to hell.)

[30] Pérouas, *La Rochelle*, pp. 228ff, 272–94, 309ff, 467ff.   [31] *Ibid.*, pp. 365, 369–72.
[32] Châtellier, *La religion des pauvres*, pp. 203–13, quotation at pp. 203–4.

In Brittany there was not the network of notaries who, I suggested last time, might make the difference between passing emotions and stable settlements; but the emotions of Bretons, even gallophone, ought not to be despised, and the missioners embedded themselves in the regional memory. Still, the guardian of the moral tradition in everyday life must generally be the *curé*, and we may wonder whether, in the days of hands-on episcopacy, of form-filling and appraisal, of the confessional-box, the catechism and the seminary, the *curé* had the time, the inclination or the capacity to do the job. The entrails, so far as one can peer into them, look relatively favourable. Sauvageon at Sennely was very involved in the settlement of his parishioners' quarrels: he says that they are not difficult to bring to agreement because they hate the law and lawyers; he also says, maybe contradicting himself, that what you have to do is to reconcile them first and absolve them in confession afterwards, otherwise 'they persist in their hatreds and are never reconciled'. Simple advice perhaps; but it might have saved a good deal of trouble if generally followed. The point, as Briggs says, was to use annual confession not as a big stick, but as 'a convenient excuse for climbing down within a social ritual which had to observe the proper order'.[33] Sauvageon was not an exceptional case. Nicole Castan has brought system to investigating the arbitration of disputes in Languedoc during the last decades of the *Ancien Régime*: she has found that, in the country, a third of the arbitrations were being done by the *curé*. He had competitors in the *seigneur* and of course the notary; against the notary he seems to have made a good deal of progress since the sixteenth century.[34]

---

[33] Briggs, *Communities of Belief*, pp. 328, 326.
[34] Nicole Castan, 'The Arbitration of Disputes under the Old Regime', in my edn of *Disputes and Settlements*, pp. 219–60.

I have tried in this lecture to distinguish the history of the moral tradition from the history of rural community. It may well be that, if we identify them, we shall find that French Catholicism had lost touch with the uirecclesiastical communities at its base, and say farewell to the moral tradition in France.[35] If we keep them apart, we seem to find that, at the Revolution, it was not dead yet.

[35] Venard, 'L'Eglise d'Avignon', pp. 1941–4, the addition about the moral tradition being my own.

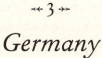

Germany

I begin my attempt to tell the story of the moral tradition in Germany with two items, both of them familiar. There is a famous illustration of it in Bernd Moeller's account of the doctrine and practice of 'sacred society' in German cities before and during the Reformation. If I may quote myself, 'it was embodied in peace and unity; it entailed some sort of covenant with the deity for the salvation of members in this world and the next; and its priests' – I should have said, 'ministers' – 'were not clerical but lay': roughly, the city fathers. Moeller took at its face value the observation that, when these cities were confronted with a choice between the old regime and the new, it was the expectation that a new order would better fulfil the objective of peace, unity, neighbourliness and brotherhood that generally carried the day for it. We may well be dealing, here, with manipulation; and on the larger front with the self-interest of patrician groups. Those probabilities do not seem to me to affect the point that we are also dealing with a manifestation, at the epicentre of the Reformation, of the moral tradition. They may, of course, make the moral tradition a less disinterested matter than I have so far suggested.[1]

---

[1] Bernd Moeller, *Imperial Cities and the Reformation* (Philadelphia, 1972; originally 1962); cf. my discussion in 'The German Reformation after Moeller', *Journal of Ecclesiastical History*, 45 (1994), pp. 673–84.

The other item is David Sabean's memorable chapter on the reception and non-reception of communion in the villages of Lutheran Württemberg sixty years later.[2] However it may have been under the pope, communion was the central matter now: its ritual form and appearance, except in one respect, was roughly traditional. It was preceded by a practice of confession reminiscent of the French local rites which were on the way out, and had their parallels in Germany. More public and collective than the Roman tradition, it certainly avoided the confessional-box; it nevertheless contained, as well as provision for private confession, enough individual attention to sinners to make it an effective rite. It seems likely that, in the country, it was not very different from what had happened before the Reformation.

As *inimicizia* in Italy, so *Feindschaft* in Germany is a structural fact of social and legal existence. In Württemberg, even more than in Lombardy, enmity is the great obstacle to communion. A man will not say his Paternoster, at mass or otherwise, because it is not in accordance with his principles to forgive his enemies without more ado; people are involved in lawsuits, to which they resort more readily than the people of Sennely, and therefore formally at enmity. They have been slandered, accused of witchcraft, unjustly punished by the authorities; are in dispute about an inheritance, at odds with their wives or husbands or the pastor. In a world of friends and enemies, they are probably more tied up with their enemies than with their friends; as Sabean says – and so does Gregory Hanlon, quoting anthropology – envy and hatred

---

[2] David Warren Sabean, *Power in the Blood: Popular Culture and Village Discourse in Early Modern Germany* (Cambridge, 1984), pp. 37–60, and, on confession, L. A. Veit, *Kirche und Volksfrömmigkeit im Zeitalter des Barock* (Freiburg i. B., 1956), pp. 6, 23–4; B. Vogler, 'La religion populaire en Allemagne luthérienne', in J. Delumeau (ed.), *Histoire vécue du peuple chrétien* (2 vols., Paris, 1979), pp. 366–72; R. Po-chia Hsia, *Social Discipline in the Reformation: Central Europe, 1580–1750* (London and New York, 1989), p. 135.

are what keep their communities together.³ Anyway they, or a lot of them, will not communicate, and their refusal sometimes goes to historic lengths; twenty-eight years in one case, a healthy example of Le Bras's 'prescription'.

As that example might indicate, the regime for persuading them to communicate is less rigorous than Borromeo's. Non-communicants are talked to a great deal, by the pastor or the mayor; they are summoned to the superintendent on his fairly frequent visitations; they generally appear, especially when they have a lawsuit behind them, tranquil and obstinate, as if conscious that their stance is supported by general opinion. They are certainly in some danger from the interconnection of church and civil power, and may be threatened with imprisonment, though it only seems to happen in very exceptional cases. They look to be in a happier position than the subjects of the Calvinist Palatinate: there, conflict-settling was virtually taken over by the prince who, dauntingly, assumed the role of the neighbour and the person to be reconciled to. In Württemberg people were virtually secure from excommunication, or the counter-reformation interdict, though they risked being refused a Christian burial. From the length of time for which many of them abstained from communion, I infer that the pastors and other authorities extended to them, as *curés* to Le Bras's 'retardataires paisibles', a fair amount of tolerance where the reason was generally judged to be honourable.⁴

I have spent a long time on this example, partly because it is so excellently done, but mainly because it is the only proper worked

---

³ Sabean, *Power in the Blood*, p. 28; Hanlon, *Confession and Community*, p. 90.
⁴ Above, chap 2, p. 40. On the Palatinate, Vogler and Estèbe, 'La genèse d'une société protestante', pp. 365–6, 378–9; V. Press, *Calvinismus und Territorialstaat* (Stuttgart, 1970), pp. 111–28, 221–46; Henry J. Cohn, 'The Territorial Princes in Germany's Second Reformation', in Menna Prestwich (ed.), *International Calvinism, 1541–1715* (Oxford, 1985), pp. 159–62.

example that we have, or rather that I know about. A recent, more conventional, investigation of the subject confirms what Sabean says.[5] In the rest of the lecture I shall be, even more than in the French case, reading it between the lines of stories about other things.

A couple of comments before I go on. Was the state of affairs in Württemberg a novelty? Sabean thinks it was: a novel intrusion of *Herrschaft* and a test of obedience.[6] This seems to be looking at it from too short a distance. I can well believe that Lutheran regimes made the relation between communion and social amity more immediate and more intense. There were now no fraternities in which to pursue one's sense of the moral tradition out of the public eye; no friars to confess to; no permissions, I think, to confess and communicate outside the parish. The frequency of communion – apparently monthly in Württemberg, three or four times a year elsewhere – was rather relentless. But from what we have seen of Italy and France it must be, essentially, the historic state of affairs; I conclude that in Germany in the late sixteenth century, the moral tradition was alive and well and living among the Lutherans.

In spite of Moeller's precedent, we ought to be a little surprised by this. Luther himself was, in theory, no friend of the moral tradition, which fell among the multifarious examples of 'works-holiness'. I think he would have rebuked the Württemberg superintendent who gave Hans Weiss the conventional warning that 'if he did not forgive, he would not receive God's mercy'. He had attempted to rewrite the Paternoster, or at least to reinterpret it, to avoid just such contractual implications. He appeared to have replaced charity by faith as the precondition for receiving

---

[5] Bruce Tolley, *Pastors and Parishioners in Württemberg during the Late Reformation* (Stanford, Calif., 1995), pp. 73, 78.
[6] Sabean, *Power in the Blood*, pp. 42–3, 58–9.

communion; he spoke of the eucharist as the sacrament of the (individual) forgiveness of sins. He removed the *pax* from the mass. 'Away with those prophets', he had written in Thesis no. 92 of the 95, 'who say to Christ's people: "peace, peace", where there is no peace.' On the face of it, he was here talking about something else; but did he not have in mind such preachers of the moral tradition as Bernardino of Siena, who certainly said: 'Peace, peace'? His doctrine of the Two Kingdoms would make one think so.[7]

I am not competent to trace the process whereby, in the face of Luther's nervousness about the moral tradition, the evangelical churches of Germany became a vehicle for it. Should we put it down to Melanchthon? To the peasants of the Peasants' War? To the accession to the evangelical ranks of conservative princes like the Brandenburgers? To Charles V and his *Interim*? To Moeller's sacred society? To *vox populi*? I don't know. But it looks to me as if, by the time of the Peace of Augsburg (1555) the Empire was divided between two moral-traditionalist confessions, and that the Evangelicals enjoyed an immense moral, as well as an increasing numerical, ascendancy over the Catholics, and not only in territories where the prince was of their persuasion.

What are we to put this down to? Seen from the angle of the rural *Gemeinden*, which had been deprived of a number of things they were partial to, like pilgrimages and holy water, the answers seem to be: communion in both kinds; the marriage of the parish clergy; and possibly the new, if it was new, practice of confession. And all of them, it seems to me, considered in the light of what they might have to contribute to the progress of the moral tradition.

---

[7] *Ibid.*, pp. 40, 51. Luther, in B. J. Kidd, *Documents of the Continental Reformation* (Oxford, 1911; repr. 1967), pp. 214 ('Shorter Catechism'), 129–30, 200 ('Pax'); John Dillenberger (ed.), *Martin Luther: Selections from his Writings* (New York, 1961), pp. 277–86 ('Babylonian Captivity'), 368–73 ('Secular Authority'), 500 ('95 Theses'); my 'The Mass as a Social Institution', p. 57.

The hostile Jesuit Peter Canisius said the attraction of the cup for the laity was that the peasants, for once, could come into contact with some real gold and thought the priests refused out of pride and dog-in-the-mangerhood. This was an ungenerous way of putting the general point that it took away one item from the separation of priest and parishioners. Did it also give them a stronger feeling of togetherness among themselves? I know nobody who actually said so, if we exclude the disgusted Giordano Bruno, who was not in Germany when he wrote the *Cena de le Ceneri*. But considering the German taste for drink, and the intimate connection of drink with the rites of sociability and reconciliation, it might be surprising if it did not. I cannot pursue that line too far, because German peasants were very hostile to the Swiss version of the eucharist, which imitated daily life more exactly; as they saw it, Zwingli wanted to deprive them of the real thing, where the pope had only deprived them of half the real thing.[8] As for clerical marriage, there was a considerable persuasion in Germany before the Reformation, and a virtually complete consensus for a long time after it, that a married clergy was a boon to community relations. Theoretically, this should perhaps have not been so, but in practice it surely was. Over confession, the odds were perhaps more even: the new system an ironing-out of some kinks on the social side (like secrecy), the old a more satisfying 'medicine', as Luther said, 'for afflicted consciences'.[9]

I have been speaking speculatively: we ought to distinguish between a claim for moral ascendancy itself, to which I can see no reasonable objection, and the reason to which I attribute it, Lutheran confiscation of the moral tradition. This account may

---

[8] Canisius, in G. Constant, *Concession à l'Allemagne de la communion sous les deux espèces* (Paris, 1923), pp. 168, 178; Giordano Bruno, *Dialoghi Italiani*, ed. G. Gentile (2 vols., Florence, 1958 edn), pp. 82–4; Vogler, 'Religion populaire', p. 370.

[9] 'Babylonian Captivity', in Dillenberger, *Luther: Selections*, p .319.

well be queried. I now approach both claims from the Catholic side, with the story of the adoption by Catholics of the Lutheran departures, communion in both kinds and the marriage of the clergy.

Both of them had been authorised by Charles V in his otherwise triumphalist *Interim* of 1548, on the grounds that there was no way of stopping them; the claim that the *Interim* was to be an instrument of peace, otherwise unconvincing, was fulfilled at least so far, and the concession was accepted by Pope Paul III.[10] After this there was a hiatus, during which the Catholic lay princes agitated for them, and the bishops resisted them; in 1562, the Emperor Ferdinand put the question about both kinds to the Council of Trent, which was narrowly persuaded not to turn him down entirely, but to remit the question to the pope, now Pius IV, Borromeo's uncle. He gave the concession on both kinds, though not on clerical marriage, in 1564. It was put into practice: briefly in Bavaria, where Duke Albert was persuaded by the Jesuits to do a U-turn; for much longer in Austria, where it went on until 1600, and in Kleve, where Duke William V adopted it during his long reign (1539–92): his motive, much influenced by the Anabaptist presence in the lower Rhineland, was to bring the 'common man' back to the 'community and churches'. For the other princes, the pressure behind the request was that the public demand for it was huge, and that it was the only way of preventing the complete disintegration of Catholicism in their

---

[10] Kidd, *Documents*, pp. 361–2; the peace motive expounded in the full version in J. Hartzheim, *Concilia Germaniae* (11 vols., Cologne, 1769–90), VI, pp. 741–2, 753 (where Luther's 'Pax, Pax' is picked up), 756. On the reception, Constant, *Concession*; A. Franzen, *Die Kelchbewegung am Niederrhein im 16ten Jahrhundert* (Münster, 1955), quotation from William V at p. 73; B. Duhr, *Geschichte der Jesuiten in den Ländern deutscher Zunge* (4 vols. in 6 parts, Freiburg i. B. and Munich, 1907–28), II/2, p. 37; L. von Pastor, *History of the Popes*, XVI (London, 1951 edn), pp. 105–40. For Austria, Constant, *Concession*, p. 726; R. J. W. Evans, *The Making of the Habsburg Monarchy* (Oxford, 1979), p. 62.

dominions. Ultramontane historians like Pastor have gloated that the outcome of the concession did not meet the expectations that had been raised: the take-up was far from universal. In Bavaria a ducal census of 1564, which was virtually a referendum, seemed to show that there were three times as many parishes that stuck to one kind as there were that accepted the new rite. There was a large number of abstentions, probably where the priest was against administration in both kinds: priests were thought to be generally hostile, on the grounds that the duke was giving the laity what, it was said, they wanted, without giving priests what *they* wanted, lawful marriage.[11] There is also the consideration that the concession was, in principle, not to parishes but to individuals, who had to ask for it when they went to confession; in quite a lot of cases it looks as if the request came from a minority of devout or snobbish or brave individuals, and caused ill-feeling among the rest.[12] As legendarily in the case of the *pax*, the instrument of reconciliation became an instrument of discord.

No concession came from Rome permitting the marriage of the clergy; but it was better established and lasted longer than communion in both kinds. It might be said that we should leave the Lutheran example out of the question, since marriage often continued the *de facto* state of pre-Reformation affairs; but the novelties of this time, the formality of marriages contracted and the number of priests marrying argue against doing so. We may give a proper discount to the statements of lay princes trying to get it legalised: one in a hundred celibate priests in the dominions of the Emperor Ferdinand, not five in the whole Duchy of Kleve. But the visitations are eloquent enough: one third of priests

---

[11] Constant, *Concession*, pp. 646–7, 397, 679 (priests, for whom also Franzen, *Kelchbewegung*, p. 70).

[12] Constant, *Concession*, pp. 345, 356, 370 and notes on statistics; Franzen, *Kelchbewegung*, pp. 57–9; J. Köhler, *Das Ringen um die Tridentinische Erneuerung im Bistum Breslau* (Cologne and Vienna, 1973), pp. 157–60.

married in the archdiocese of Cologne in 1536; the same in Trier in the 1570s; half in Speyer in the 1580s – the villages say their priests are pious and bring up their children well. In Münster diocese, one third of priests married in the 1570s, which is standard until 1650. In Silesia, 20 per cent: one might have thought it would have been higher, for in this area of fragmented authority the *Gemeinden* or the nobility are in charge and if, say the church authorities, you do anything about it they will simply turn Lutheran. In Alsace nearly a century later, much the same state of affairs, though more clandestinity is now required. In 1700 the pope writes to the archbishop of Mainz to try to persuade him that concubinary priests should at least not be given parishes.[13] We are not dealing here with an 'abuse', or not mainly: we are dealing with the judgements of rural communities about what is the sensible, indeed the Christian, thing; encouraged, at least before 1600, by many of their princes, and given confidence by the Lutheran example. It was not only the Lutherans who, as Robert Scribner has explained, took Luther to be a saint: there were priests in Bavaria who, according to the Jesuits, thought so too – 'den heiligen Dr Martinus und edlen Mann Gottes' (the saintly doctor and noble man of God Dr Martinus).[14]

The U-turn in Bavaria over the chalice was mainly the work of the Jesuit Peter Canisius; it signified the appearance of the Society of Jesus as a principal performer on the German stage. In Italy, to our surprise, we have found the Jesuits to be something of a pillar of the moral tradition; in France, where this does not

---

[13] Constant, *Concession*, pp. 442–3; Franzen, in E. W. Zeeden and H. Molitor, *Die Visitation im Dienste der kirchlichen Reform* (Münster, 1967), p. 17; Köhler, *Breslau*, pp. 187–94; Becker-Huberti (below, n. 27), pp. 166–7; Forster (below, n. 17), pp. 22–8; Châtellier (below, n. 25), pp. 176–82; Ortner (below, n. 30), pp. 60ff; Owen Chadwick, *The Popes and European Revolution* (Oxford, 1981), p. 111.

[14] R. W. Scribner, 'Incombustible Luther', *Past and Present*, no. 110 (1986), pp. 38–68, and in his *Popular Culture and Popular Movements in Reformation Germany* (London and Ronceverte, 1987), pp. 323–53; Duhr, *Jesuiten*, I, p. 472.

quite appear, we are to associate the tradition, if not with them, at least with the anti-Jansenist front. We shall look hard before we find anything similar in Germany, and certainly shall not find it in the story of communion in both kinds. From the general Laínez downwards, the Society was a bitter enemy of giving the cup to the laity. There is wonderful comedy in its wriggling to evade the decision of a pope whom it was supposed to be committed to obeying; there is also something heroic about its resistance to the wishes of princes on whom it depended. I can think of two reasons for this, one obvious, one more occult. Ignatius's principle of not doing or saying anything against established Catholic practice proved stronger than loyalty to the pope: since to concede the cup was to recognise Lutheran moral ascendancy, it must be wrong in itself, and those who wanted it could not be real Catholics.[15] The more occult reason was that Jesuits had a devotional ear for the sacraments and were virtually tone deaf to the appeal of communion, in one kind or both, as an instrument of sacred society. No slippery slope of Moellerism for them. Missions and fraternities indeed, but of a kind. The rural missions, which were being pushed from headquarters from the 1590s, took Roman orthodoxy and frequent communion into the muddle of village Catholicism: they did not come to bring peace. There were plenty of them in Bavaria, but the only peacemaking mission I can find occurred after 1713, when the object was to reconcile enmities arising from the War of the Spanish Succession, in which Bavaria and Austria had taken different sides.[16] In the cities the Jesuit sodality or congregation, with its frequent confession and communion, its works of charity and its networking under

---

[15] *Spiritual Exercises*, 'Rules for Thinking with the Church', nos. 6–9 (my edn by T. Corbishley, Wheathampstead, 1973, pp. 120–1); Duhr, *Jesuiten*, I, pp. 447–9; Constant, *Concession*, p. 346.

[16] Duhr, *Jesuiten*, I, pp. 468–72; Châtellier, *La religion des pauvres*, pp. 108ff.

the patronage of a belligerent Mary, was a fraternity turned inside-out. One of the founders of the sodalities in Germany, Jakob Rem, was also the prophet of a 'bloody but holy' war against the Protestants in the years before 1618: in the time of triumph which followed, Jesuits and jackboots restored the rule of Rome in conquered territories like Silesia.[17]

This is a sharp picture, and we shall want to make some qualification to it. But at the height of Jesuit influence in the Empire, between 1560 and 1630, it does not seem too much to regard the Society as a machine for the impoverishment of the moral tradition among Catholics, and for its extinction in so far as it entailed a respect for Lutheran achievements in maintaining it. We may wish to sympathise with the bishop of Speyer, a noble bishop of the old school, who said to the Lutheran councillors of his city that 'he wished the devil would take all Jesuits'.[18]

Ronald Po-chia Hsia has documented the clash between Catholic civic tradition and Jesuit innovation in the city of Münster: the Jesuits came to Westphalia as outsiders who drank wine instead of beer and spoke high German instead of low.[19] That should have helped them in the Rhineland and the south. But what do we find there? We find an extraordinarily fierce argument going on in the Jesuit provinces about music. The working Jesuits in Vienna, Bavaria and the Rhineland were the objects of a tug-of-war between their superiors and their lay constituency. According to the Jesuit constitutions, said the superiors, there must be virtually no music in Jesuit churches: no chanted offices,

---

[17] Louis Châtellier, *The Europe of the Devout* (Cambridge and Paris, 1989), pp. 1–46; Marc Forster, *The Counter-Reformation in the Villages: Religion and Reform in the Diocese of Speyer, 1560–1720* (Ithaca, N.Y., and London, 1992), pp. 124–6. On Rem, Châtellier, *Europe*, see index; and Prosperi, 'Il missionario', p. 207. On Silesia, Châtellier, *La religion des pauvres*, p. 47.

[18] Forster, *Counter-Reformation*, p. 48.

[19] *Society and Religion in Münster, 1535–1618* (New Haven and London, 1984), pp. 87–92.

of course, but no high masses either; certainly not with musical settings, and especially not with instruments. More: the constitutions appeared to say that Jesuits were not to have musical instruments in their houses; were not to sing madrigals; not to buy sheet music or accept it as a present, even when it was on sacred texts; not to copy or compose it without express permission from the provincial. These instructions came from Paul Hoffaeus, German assistant to the general Acquaviva, in 1596: Hoffaeus also banned polyphonic music from the chapel of the English College in Rome, which the Jesuits controlled. This at a time when Lassus was in his prime in Munich; and when Lutherans were posting to Venice to import the latest thrilling innovations from St Mark's. Lucky Henry Garnet to be safe in England, playing the organ with William Byrd in country houses! Of course, the superiors could not win: after a heroic dispute about the organ of the Jesuit church in Vienna, reminiscent of the nineteenth-century argument about the Brunswick Methodist Chapel in Leeds, Acquaviva caved in.[20] Polyphony was a very long way from the concerns of rural communities, but I take it to have in Germany somewhat the status of banditry in Italy, as symbol and symptom of the moral tradition. When we come as we must to the tragedy of Jesuit politics in the Empire, we may remember that harmony was not the Society's forte.

I say without apology 'Jesuit' politics. When the Empire lurched into disaster in the first decades of the seventeenth century, I doubt if the Society as such *had* a policy, as it had under Acquaviva in the last period of the French wars of religion. In Germany individual Jesuits took different views about politics,

---

[20] Duhr, *Jesuiten*, I, pp. 442–6; L. Hicks (ed.), *Letters and Memorials of Robert Persons*, I (Catholic Record Society, XXXIX, 1942), p. 312; J. Kerman, *The Masses and Motets of William Byrd* (London and Boston, 1981), pp. 49–50; W. R. Ward, *Religion and Society in England, 1790–1850* (London, 1972), pp. 144–6.

as they did about music, witches and the taking of interest. But the drift of Jesuit doings here since the days of Canisius had been fairly unmistakable, and it is not unreasonable to take the two Jesuit confessors Lamormaini and Contzen, who served Ferdinand II of Austria and Maximilian of Bavaria respectively, as representative of it. The consciences of these cousins were a pushover for confessors who gave them a hard and expansionist idea of the responsibilities of a Catholic prince.[21]

Politically speaking, it seems rather obvious what their optimal policy was: to be nice to the Lutherans, if not at home, then as represented by the elector of Saxony (and the elector of Brandenburg, though here the relation was more complicated because the elector was personally a Calvinist, though, one may say, politically a Lutheran). The Saxons had always taken a conciliatory view of the implications of the Peace of Augsburg; they were now under heavy pressure from the forces of the Calvinist international acting from the Rhine Palatinate. Their price was modest: a legitimation of the *status quo* in the northern and north-western German bishoprics which since 1555 were either in their hands, or subject to gentlemanly processes of alternation between Lutheran and Catholic electees. Some of them, one may add, like Halberstadt and Osnabrück, were the refuge of an agreeably muddled syncretism.[22]

On the Catholic side, many or most influential people thought that the Lutherans ought to be accommodated: they included

---

[21] Robert Bireley, *Maximilian von Bayern, Adam Contzen S. J. und die Gegenreformation in Deutschland, 1624–1635* (Göttingen, 1975); *idem, Religion and Politics in the Age of the Counter-Reformation: Emperor Ferdinand II, William Lamormaini and the Formation of Imperial Policy* (Chapel Hill, 1981); *idem, The Counter-Reformation Prince* (Chapel Hill and London, 1990), pp. 157–60.

[22] Saxon politics: Simon Adams, 'The Union, the League and the Politics of Europe', in Geoffrey Parker, *The Thirty Years' War* (London, 1984), pp. 25–38 and Pastor, *History of the Popes*, XX, pp. 243, 249, 375, XXIII, pp. 332–4. Bishoprics and syncretism: *ibid.*, XX, p. 295 (Halberstadt) and in general 284–353; Hsia, *Social Discipline*, p. 132 (Osnabrück).

a majority of the lay councillors of Ferdinand and Maximilian. To no avail. Pressed by Lamormaini, Ferdinand's conscience required him to issue the Edict of Restitution of 1629; pressed by Contzen, Maximilian's conscience, quite against his political interests, which were to be civil to the other electors in order to secure the confirmation of his electoral rank, required him to go along with it. In Vienna, Lamormaini gloated over the four new Jesuit provinces, the *ninety* new Jesuit colleges, which would arise to 'reform religion' in the north: that is, to dragoon the Lutherans back to Catholicism. What idiocy! What hubris! Nemesis struck soon enough in the person of King Gustav Adolf; the prudent Ferdinand III made his peace with the Lutherans at Prague in 1636. It would be too strong to say that Lamormaini dragged the Jesuits down with him in his disgrace; it does not seem too strong to say that thereafter they no longer held a moral ascendancy on the Catholic side.[23]

After this digression, I return to the parish pump, this time a Catholic pump (probably miraculous), to see how the *Gemeinden* were getting on, and what became of them. My knowledge extends to four or five areas, and my search for the moral tradition attracts me to two of them: the diocese and territory of Speyer in the Rhineland; and the diocese of Strasburg, meaning rural Alsace (I should say, Elsass). In Speyer we come across a powerful special element of the German situation, which might perhaps have been mentioned before: the diocese/territory is run by the cathedral chapter, noble of course and so far as I can see unreformed throughout. We meet no tough bishops like Julius Echter in Würzburg, and outside the city no Jesuits. From a remarkably relaxed set of visitations during the 1580s we get a clear snapshot of how things are on the ground. The *Gemeinde* is in charge of the parish and the priest: if it does not exactly appoint him, it

---

[23] Bireley, *Lamormaini*, pp. 134, 209ff; Forster, *Counter-Reformation*, p. 217.

gives him a tough examination; it tells him what feasts to observe; it taxes him. It protects his generally respectable marital and domestic life; he farms, is said to behave in a neighbourly way, has a reasonable or excessive devotion to wine. They, and he, keep a traditional local ritual; they have not heard of the marriage decree of Trent or the confessional-box. Their practice of confession at Easter ('in the sacristy, as is the custom with the heretics') is either Lutheran, or traditional, or both.

A century passes. Things have moved on a little: the people, says Marc Forster, now describe themselves as Catholics rather than as Christians. The *Gemeinden*, still in charge, will not now allow concubinary priests; they have adopted the Tridentine law of marriage and the confessional-box; they will not let Protestants settle in or marry into the villages. Something has happened, it seems by inter-generational osmosis; the people appear as happy with the new regime as with the old.[24]

What we do not get from Forster is any direct light on the history of the moral tradition. But here we can get something from the very delicate investigation of Catholic Alsace/Elsass by Louis Châtellier. In general it is much the same story, at least for the decades from 1660 to 1680, where he starts.[25] A cathedral chapter at the top, *Gemeinden* at the bottom together run a historic 'nébuleuse', not a Borromean, even Federico Borromean, parish. There are Jesuits around, but they mainly act by fostering real fraternities, which are popular and built on old foundations, like the crossbow-shooters' fraternity dedicated to – Guess who? – St Sebastian. At two points in Châtellier's exposition I prick up my ears. There are virtually no registers, he says, until the 1680s: the *Pfarrer* think of the flock as families, not as individuals.

---

[24] Forster, *Counter-Reformation*, especially chaps. 1–2, 6–7.
[25] Louis Châtellier, *Tradition chrétienne et renouveau catholique dans l'ancienne diocèse de Strasbourg* (Paris, 1981), chaps. 2, 4, 5.

We are a long way from the *status animarum*. About confession, accordingly, he has the feeling that 'the sacrament of penance is administered much more to a collectivity taken as a whole, than to separate individuals'.[26] Do I not detect my moral tradition? Should we not, if we could go into it, find a state of affairs much like the one across the Rhine in Württemberg? Yes, if we may judge from Trevor Johnson's thesis on the (re)catholicisation of the Upper Palatinate after the Bavarian conquest of 1621. There, he says, the story about enmity and communion is just the same in the cautious new Catholic regime as it had been in the Lutheran regime before it.[27]

Châtellier's *nébuleuse* ceased to twinkle when Louis XIV took over, and a squadron of ecclesiastical carpet-baggers was parachuted in from Paris.[28] Native bishops might act to much the same effect, like Christoph Bernhard von Galen, elected bishop of Münster shortly after the peace of 1648. Von Galen was not your standard counter-reformation worthy: he was mainly occupied in fighting, and fought two wars, one against his episcopal city and one against the Dutch, to whom he was known as 'Bommer-Berend'. As bishop, he was a Borromean caricature. He held forty-three synods in twenty-seven years, though too busy to appear at more than one of them; his proforma for the *status animarum* ran to seven detailed sections, and puts Giberti and Borromeo in the shade. He banned the usual public confession, which was in the Münster ritual, and brought in the confessional-box, where people shifted about not knowing what to say. He

---

[26] *Ibid.*, pp. 46, 131, 140, 190–1, 244.

[27] Trevor Johnson, 'The Recatholicisation of the Upper Palatinate, 1621–c. 1700' (Cambridge University PhD thesis, 1992), p. 182; Manfred Becker-Huberti, *Die Tridentinische Reform im Bistum Münster unter Furstbischof Christoph Bernhard von Galen, 1650–1678* (Münster, 1978), p. 242 – refusal of Easter communion due to 'Streitigkeiten' punished by a fine, 1624 – a rare reference.

[28] Châtellier, *Strasbourg*, pp. 209ff.

brought in marriage according to Trent and the Roman ritual, which backfired when the marriage-feasters were obliged to bring themselves, their drink and their folk customs into church. The big success he claimed was to have extirpated clerical marriage in ten years by imprisoning, flogging and exiling priests' partners; according to one of his successors he persuaded the priests to sin more prudently in future.[29]

We must take it that Catholic Westphalia survived von Galen, as Catholic and Lutheran Alsace survived Louis XIV. It did not survive in a good deal of the archbishopric of Salzburg, where the expulsion in 1731 of 20,000 mountaineers who had just formally declared themselves Lutheran provided the eighteenth century with its most recent example of Catholic bigotry. For how long before that the people of the valleys had actually thought of themselves as Protestants is a debatable and perhaps meaningless question. They had been at enmity with the archbishops since the Peasants' War of 1525, which had been brutally put down; and the archbishops had used the weapons of counter-reformation episcopacy in the attempt to bring them to heel. With no success: in the 1560s they rebelled in defence of communion in both kinds, to which the archbishop was frantically hostile; in the 1680s 30 per cent of their children were said to be illegitimate, which must mean that the archbishop had adopted the Tridentine law of marriage, and they had rejected it. The priests, whose only fault in the good old days before 1525 had been setting up bars on feast days in competition with the innkeepers, had turned into government informers, traitors to the valley communities and to community itself. In one case, the people said they had given 200 days' work building the priest a house, and that was what they had got for their pains; if they had been able to provide him

---

[29] Becker-Huberti, *Münster*, pp. 81, 106 (synods), 279, 242 (*status animarum*), 229–37 (confession), 264–70 (marriage), 165–76 (clerical marriage).

with a wife, they might have been able to get a better grip on him.[30]

If we want to get out of these instances a story of the moral tradition in Catholic Germany, we shall have to go carefully. One step I cannot take here, as I have done in Italy and France, is to invoke the rural missions as giving it a shot in the arm towards the close of our period. There is indeed one region where it looks very likely that this happened; a word about it will balance the sad story of the Salzburgers. During the 1690s the Italian Jesuits began to extend their missions into the Swiss Catholic cantons: their system of mass penances and scenes of universal reconcilia-tion went down very well in the mountains, and they found indigenous Jesuits with the talent to continue them.[31] After this, standing Jesuit 'missions' were set up in neighbouring parts to cater for the people of the remoter valleys; one of them settled in the Tyrol. Here the missions did nothing dramatic, and we do not hear much about them settling feuds: they turned up regularly, preached and confessed, brought medicines and worked to set up proper churches. Presence and affection do seem, in this case, to have worked wonders:[32] it is true that the history of the Tyrolese, in and since the Peasants' War, had been a great deal happier than that of the Salzburgers. In Germany proper the 'Italian method' was tried, but did not come off: perhaps the people liked it, but most of the German Jesuits, and especially the Catholic princes, did not: not our sort of thing, too much noise and excitement, it drove people mad, they said. We can find a calmer version of it being tried here and there, as in Bamberg in 1738, where the

---

[30] Franz Ortner, *Reformation, katholische Reform und Gegenreformation im Erzstift Salzburg* (Salzburg, 1981), pp. 34–40, 60–2 (good old days), 69–78, 96 (both kinds), 102, 142 (marriage), 185, 195–203 (spies, etc.). Hsia, *Social Discipline*, pp. 51–2, 63–70.

[31] Duhr, *Jesuiten*, III, p. 676, IV/2, pp. 191–3, 229–31; Châtellier, *Religion des pauvres*, pp. 205–8.

[32] Duhr, *Jesuiten*, IV/2, pp. 231–7 (235, feuds, 236, medicine).

mission ended with everyone kissing a crucifix as a pax, and perhaps in Alsace; but a more characteristic invention of the eighteenth-century missions was the collective first communion, a feast of youthful piety not of charity, which appears about 1750.[33]

So we are sent back to the mysterious everyday history of the rural *Gemeinde*, and must make the best of what shafts of light we have. It looks as if the Thirty Years War was some kind of watershed. On the up-side of it, the state of affairs seems pretty clear: Lutheran moral ascendancy, and Catholic accommodation to Lutheran inventions thought to be beneficial to the moral tradition; Jesuit attempts to dam the current, promoting disaster. On the down-side, one of the few obvious things is that Catholic Germany managed to become a lot more confident about itself, and modestly to thrive within the established boundaries. What are we to say about this? If it were simply conformity to the state, as theories of confessionalisation imply, I do not see how Catholic Germany would have avoided the fate of much of Catholic France, which it seems to have done. At a guess, and over a long time, my suppositions would be: some assimilation in rural communities of the devotional attitude to the sacraments, hence a success for the Jesuits; some extrapolation of togetherness away from the sacraments and into, for example, collective pilgrimage to local shrines; some shifting towards, or perhaps just a solid persistence in, the thaumaturgical, the non-social miracle.

---

[33] *Ibid.*, pp. 200, 205, 210 (Bamberg), 222–5; 204, 205, 241 (first communions); Châtellier, *Religion des pauvres*, p. 208 (Alsace).

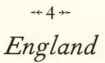

4

England

I come home to England, and offer two quotations to start with. The first is from Thomas Cranmer's preface to the communion service in his *Book of Common Prayer* (1549):

> The same order [as with sexual offences] shall the curate use with those betwixt whom he shall perceive malice and hatred to reign, not suffering then to be partakers of the Lord's Table until he know them to be reconciled. And if one of the parties so at variance be content to forgive from the bottom of his heart all that the other hath trespassed against him, and the other party will not be persuaded to a godly unity, but remain still in his frowardness and malice; the Minister in that case ought to admit the penitent person to the Holy Communion, and not him that is obstinate.[1]

The second, a pair, is from Thomas Watson, *A Holsome and Catholic Doctrine* (1558):

> Of confession to a man's neighbour whom he hath offended: 'Because God is charity, and the God of peace and not of dissension, and doth not vouchsafe to pour his grace into that heart where hatred, enmity and breach of peace remaineth; therefore no man can be reconciled to God, whom he hath by his sin offended, that is

---

[1] In the version I have to hand, *The First Prayer Book of King Edward VI, 1549* (London, 1888), p. 192; *The Second . . . 1552* (London, 1888), p. 157. Susan Brigden, 'Religious and Social Obligation in Early 16th-Century London', *Past and Present*, no. 103 (1984), pp. 67–112, is a wonderful account of the status of the obligation of charity in everyday life.

not reconciled to his brother or neighbour whom by some injury either in word or deed he hath likewise offended.' On communion: 'This is the mystery of peace and the unity of Christ's mystical body; and he that receiveth the mystery of unity and keepeth not the bond of peace and unity, he receiveth not the mystery for himself, but a testimony against himself. Therefore of all things let us be sure of this, that we be in charity, and that no anger fret us, no pride inflame us, nor no envy torment our hearts, when we come to our Lord's table.'[2]

Two minds with a single thought, so it seems, perhaps a single cliché: as Richard Baxter was to say, the trouble with talking about peace and unity is that it is hard to find anybody who is against it.[3] But neither passage is, I think, clichaic. Cranmer had certainly come through Luther's worry about the moral tradition and, despite the quotation (which may indeed not be Cranmer's own), I am not sure that he was quite reconciled to it. Retranslation of some of its essential texts had become something of a preoccupation for early English reformers. Tyndale, translating the Sermon on the Mount in 1526, had englished: 'Blessed are the maintainers of peace', by whom the reader was surely to understand the secular authorities. He changed back to the usual 'peacemakers' later. His version of the angelic salutation to the shepherds removed the offering of peace on earth to men of goodwill; Cranmer's, in the *Gloria* of his communion service, was of course 'in earth peace, goodwill toward men'. This was a blow at the traditional interpretation of the angels' message, and to the idea that there was something transcendental about peacemaking. The blow was repeated, or so I understand it, in his prayer for

---

[2] Watson, fols. lxxi[r], lxiiii[r]: taken from Lucy Wooding, 'From Humanists to Heretics: English Catholic Theology and Ideology, c. 1530–c. 1570' (Oxford University DPhil thesis, 1995), p. 102.

[3] *The Reformed Pastor* (1656; abridged edn, Edinburgh, 1862; repr. Edinburgh, 1974), chap. 3, section 1.4.

peace at evensong; this he rewrote so as to exclude exterior peace, the *pax temporis*, as the object of prayer. He replaced it by 'rest and quietness' which, if it means anything about the external world, is surely the equivalent of *tranquillitas*. There is no *pax* ritual in his liturgies: the congregation does not become 'apt for the most holy mysteries'. I take it that we are to read behind these careful alterations the influence of his mature predestinarian theology and receptionist view of the eucharist: that Cranmer nevertheless, in his service as well as in his rules for communicating, repeated the peace motif in a fairly strong verbal form may be one of the ways in which his liturgies made concessions to tradition that he himself did not fancy. Watson, for his part, also made gestures towards the middle ground (confession to the neighbour, 'mystery' not sacrament, Lord's table); but he had behind him a confident tradition, which included the deadly sins, and a regime persuaded that peace and unity was the line to take. He tapped a vein of eloquence, which Cranmer here was not required to do.[4]

Perhaps it is silly of me to envisage the history of Christianity in England in the century or so after 1558 as a sort of competition between two or more parties for the prize of representing the moral tradition. But this is roughly what I shall be doing in this lecture. I start with the Church of England, considered as a single entity. One consequence of coming to the English case after a tour of the continent is that one becomes aware how very strong and direct the English evidence is. In the last lecture particularly I have often had to look below the surface, peel off layers,

---

[4] William Tyndale, *New Testament, 1534*, ed. N. Hardy Wallis (Cambridge, 1938), pp. x, 127 (Luke 2. 14); *Prayer Book, 1549*, p. 194, *1552*, p. 170; Diarmaid MacCulloch, *Thomas Cranmer: A Life* (New Haven and London, 1996), pp. 418–19, and see index *s.v.* eucharist, predestination. My interpretation, rashly, differs from MacCulloch's. The traditional 'Exhortation to those negligent to come to the Communion' of 1549 was sidetracked and toned down in 1552 (*Prayer Book, 1549*, pp. 197–8, *1552*, pp. 163–5). Eamon Duffy, *The Stripping of the Altars* (New Haven and London, 1992), pp. 93, 531–6 for the other side.

extrapolate from famous cases, infer what was felt from what was done. I do not think it is simply familiarity which makes the English evidence seem so rich: speaking for myself, and more than a little nervously in present company, I am not sure that I *am* more familiar with it. But it seems to jump out at one: most of it comes from the established church, and I do not think this is simply because it *is* the established church.

Clerical biographers rarely let pass the opportunity of telling us that their subjects devoted a great deal of time to the arbitration of disputes; real life seems to bear them out. To start with, there is Bernard Gilpin, whose doings as a peacemaker in the Northumbrian badlands first introduced me to the subject. A *protégé* of Cuthbert Tunstall, and a learned traditionalist who objected impartially to transubstantiation and the Genevan discipline as jumped-up inventions, his annual missions to the land of 'deadly feod' began under Mary and continued under Elizabeth: they seem to show a perfect consciousness of what he was doing. His famous intervention between the parties while preaching in Rothbury church could easily have come from one of Vincent de Paul's priests in Corsica a century later; except perhaps for the realistic note that he failed to persuade them to a *pax*, only to a truce to last as long as he was around.[5] At the other end of the Elizabethan spectrum we have the ministers of the Dedham classis, grappling with enmity and refusal of the sacrament, and as happy with Cranmer's preface as they were unhappy with his service. To Master Catlin in Wenham, in 1588, asking whether he could admit to communion two people in hatred against one another for words defamatory about a dead sheep, 'it was

---

[5] Patrick Collinson, *The Religion of Protestants* (Oxford, 1982), pp. 45, 109–11; *idem*, *Archbishop Grindal* (London, 1979), pp. 131–43, 271–2; G. Carleton, *Vita Bernardi Gilpini* (London, 1628), pp. 9–10, 18–19, 25–6, 29, 53; cf. my 'The Counter-Reformation and the People of Catholic Europe', p. 55; D. Marcombe, 'Bernard Gilpin: Anatomy of an Elizabethan Legend', *Northern History*, 16 (1980), pp. 20–39.

answered that if they would profess love to one another he might, because he cannot *work* love but only admonish them of the danger of it; but if they be in open hatred the booke [of Common Prayer] warrants him not to receive them'. During the Civil War it was alleged, with what truth I do not know, that the common lawyers in Parliament fell out with the Presbyterian clergy 'not so much upon conscience, as upon fear that the Presbytery spoil their market, and take up most of the country pleas without law'.[6] This had been Paleotti's problem in Bologna.

Among the laity the seriousness of communion as a moral occasion emerges from everywhere you look. In Susan Brigden's 1520s London Joanna Carpenter tugs at the sleeve of a neighbour kneeling at the altar, to tell her that she was not entitled to receive her 'rights' until she had asked her, Joanna's, forgiveness for a trespass against her. In Donald Spaeth's Wiltshire of the 1670s a parish refuses to receive communion from the parson, whom they regard as unfit to administer it because he pursues them with hostility and lawsuits. We ought to remember his suggestion about the continuing strength, as in Lutheran Germany, of the doctrine of the *manducatio impiorum* – that those who eat and drink unworthily eat and drink judgement unto themselves – which was one of the things Cranmer had retained in the Prayer Book though he did not believe it himself. Between the two it has been possible to assemble a rich harvest of documentation for pre-communion peacemaking.[7] It represents ministers of all

[6] R. G. Usher (ed.), *The Presbyterian Movement in the Reign of Queen Elizabeth* (Camden Society, 3rd series VIII, 1905), p. 71; Keith Thomas, *Religion and the Decline of Magic* (London, 1973 edn), pp. 182–3, 631.

[7] Susan Brigden, *London and the Reformation* (Oxford, 1989), p. 28; Donald A. Spaeth, 'Common Prayer? Popular Observance of the Anglican Liturgy in Restoration Wiltshire', in S. J. Wright (ed.), *Parish, Church and People* (London, 1988), pp. 125–51 (135–6 for *manducatio impiorum*, and cf. Sabean, *Power in the Blood*, pp. 41, 44–5); MacCulloch, *Cranmer*, pp. 405–6, 463–4, 621; Arnold Hunt, 'The Lord's Supper in Early Modern England', forthcoming in *Past and Present*.

parties and, on the literary side at least, more of it is about the godly than the others. I shall be saying something about this later in the lecture; for the time being I venture the thought that the most obvious flaw of a godly or simply diligent parish clergy, from the point of view of the moral tradition, was administering communion too often, and with inadequate notice. 'I know by the canons [of 1604]', said a churchwarden, 'we ought to have a week's warning; . . . it is not like a muster, no more but beat up the drum and come away; they ought to have more time.'[8] In the moral tradition time was of the essence, and a week not a long time.

What, if anything, was lost to the peacemaking process by the absence of a rite of confession, old or new, was made up for by the doings of the church courts. From Ralph Houlbrooke, Martin Ingram and Jim Sharpe we find plentifully exemplified, in cases ranging over matrimony, defamation and inheritance, the twelfth-century dictum that 'pactum legem vincit et amor judicium' (agreement conquers law, and love judgement). Village elders, on their own or with the help of parson, gentry and others, find these courts a serviceable medium for ensuring, at least for settled inhabitants, the primacy of neighbourly ethics, of arbitration over judgement. Under the umbrella of the courts, four honest neighbours sit down to settle a dispute on All Souls' Day in the church at Egton in the cowboy country of the Yorkshire moors. Two women from another part of Yorkshire, divided by gossip about sexual adventures, are made 'lovers and friends' by another woman: for such cases, I must surely withdraw what I said about women as unlikely peacemakers. The parties eat and drink together and, in the conventional but none the less moving phrase, end 'all actions, suites and controversies whatsoever

[8] Martin Ingram, *Church Courts, Sex and Marriage in England, 1570–1640* (Cambridge, 1987), p. 121.

from the beginning of the world until [this] time'.[9] Nor were the doings of the secular law outside the orbit of the moral tradition: William Lambarde expounded it to the justices of the peace in Kent, and Sir Richard Grosvenor, in Cheshire, pursued it in a most committed and sensitive style as 'the Christian way' towards 'heavenly peace'. Like Federico Borromeo, he was virtually quoting William Durandus: 'ut de pace temporis, per pacem pectoris, transeamus ad pacem aeternitatis' (so that from external peace, through the peace of the heart, we may pass over to the peace of eternity).[10]

It seems as if one might go on forever; but I cannot leave the moral tradition in the Church of England without a word about two classic expositions of it which everybody has heard of: George Gifford's *Brief Discourse of . . . the Country Divinity* of 1582, and George Herbert's *A Priest to the Temple* of fifty years later.

Gifford was the parson of Maldon in Essex, and his dialogue is a satire on the moral tradition from the point of view of a minister committed to godliness. One of the many remarkable things about it is that, at least to a modern ear, he makes his defender of the moral tradition, the parishioner Atheos, more attractive than his opponent, the parson Zelotes. Atheos is a rural traditionalist who sticks up for his old-style curate Sir Robert as the best priest

[9] R. Houlbrooke, *Church Courts and the People during the English Reformation* (Oxford, 1979), index under 'peaceful settlement of disputes' and table, pp. 275–7; Martin Ingram, 'Communities and Courts: Law and Disorder in Early 17th Century Wiltshire', in J. S. Cockburn (ed.), *Crime in England, 1550–1800* (London, 1977), pp. 110–34, and Ingram, *Church Courts*, pp. 30ff, 295–316; J. A. Sharpe, 'Such Disagreement Betwixt Neighbours: Litigation and Human Relations in Early Modern England', in Bossy, *Disputes and Settlements*, pp. 167–88, quoted at pp. 174, 176; Michael Clanchy, 'Law and Love in the Middle Ages', in *ibid.*, pp. 47–67.

[10] Steve Hindle, 'The Keeping of the Public Peace', in P. Griffiths *et al.* (eds.), *The Experience of Authority in Early Modern England* (London, 1996), pp. 213–48, especially pp. 228–9, 232, 238; William Durandus, *Rationale Divinorum Officiorum* (Naples, 1859 edn), p. 249, and my 'The Mass as a Social Institution', p. 54.

in the country, a good fellow. But does he, asks Zelotes, reprove naughtiness? 'Yea, that he doth', says Atheos, 'for if there be any that do not agree, he will seek for to make them friends: for he will get them to play a game or two at Bowls or Cards, and to drink together at the alehouse. I think it a godly way to make charity.' There are a lot of good lines in the piece, and Atheos gets quite a few of them. Are we to think that Gifford is more divided in his mind than he seems? Surely not; but there must be something worrying him. Why, otherwise, would he so deftly skate over the problem in the Paternoster? He complains that the purported Christianity of Atheos does not extend to a genuine taking on board of the petitions 'Hallowed be thy name' and 'Thy will be done.' True enough. But then: 'I might go through all the petitions and find the same.' Well, no. If he had got as far as 'Forgive us our trespasses' he would have found Atheos on pretty safe ground.[11]

In Herbert's case we have no such backchat, and no dilemmas. He was an excellent Protestant. He came out of the same stable as Philip Sidney; and he may be particularly remembered here as an alumnus and fellow of Trinity and a reader in rhetoric in this university. Well, on my vote, Trinity and Cambridge would get the Nobel Prize of the moral tradition. If there is anything like *A Priest to the Temple* in the literature of seventeenth-century Europe, I have not come across it. You may say: he is against drink and the alehouse. Yes, for good or ill, for the parson; no, for the laity, to whom his very useful injunction is 'Drink not the third glass.' He is somewhat against priestly marriage, preferring celibacy on his own account, though marriage on the

---

[11] *A Briefe Discourse of Certaine Points of the Religion, which is Among the Common Sort of Christians, which may be Termed, the Countrie Divinitie* (London, 1582), fols. 2^r and 1^r–7^r in general, 71^r–72^r, 46^v; Collinson, *Religion of Protestants*, pp. 103–4, 108; Christopher Haigh, *English Reformations* (Oxford, 1993), pp. 281–2.

parish's. He is as devout as Ignatius, and perhaps from similar sources like the *Imitation of Christ*; but he is as social as the Piovano Arlotto. For charity's sake he prefers common prayer to solitary:

> Though private prayer be a brave designe,
> Yet publick hath more promises, more love.

What I like best about him is his conviction that neighbourhood, charity, community entail hard work, but not in our sense social work or works of mercy. Would he have agreed with the ministers at Dedham that the parson 'cannot *work* love'? He knows that his parson is standing in a minefield and that defusing the mines and turning the field to crops is a dangerous venture and requires patience. His work is socialising, inviting round ('Countrey people are very observant of such things, and will not be perswaded, but being not invited, they are hated'); arbitrating with the parish elders, preaching by friendliness. He is keen on collective occasions, like the Rogation procession; his task is to make sure that, when the parish assembles for such events, it actually does so as a whole, because potential absentees have been eased, perhaps nagged, out of their resentments. His community is not magic, but a social miracle. 'Love your neighbour, yet pull not down your hedge.'[12] It is nice to see him agreeing with Robert Frost's wall-sharer, that good fences make good neighbours. It is true that Herbert was only a country parson himself for three years before he died; but we have good authority for believing

---

[12] *A Priest to the Temple: Or, The Countrey Parson in his Character and Rule of Holy Life* (1632; 1st published in Herbert's *Remains*, London, 1652; repr. Menston, Yorks., 1970), chaps. 3, 8, 9, 11, 23, 25, etc. *Jacula Prudentum*, also in the *Remains*, p. 9; cf. other saws pp. 45 ('Where there is peace, God is'), 16 ('An ill agreement is better than a good judgment'). 'The Church-Porch', stanzas 5–8, 67, in L. Martz (ed.), *George Herbert* (Oxford, 1994), pp. 3, 15. Note the 'Finis' of Herbert's poem collection *The Temple* (1633): 'Glory be to *God* on high / And on earth peace / Goodwill toward men.'

that his model was close enough to real life in the Wiltshire of his time.[13]

We cannot now explore the Catholic part in the English Post-Reformation without being actively aware that we have two sorts of Catholic to talk about: the recusants and the church papists. The simple question will be, whether we are to equate these two with Counter-Reformation and moral tradition respectively. Christopher Haigh has inhibited a simple answer to the question by demonstrating that, in Lancashire at any rate, recusancy and community may have gone together in wholesale parish dissidence from the Elizabethan church; and where we have community we probably have the moral tradition.[14] I shall none the less proceed, so far as I may, on the assumption that the answer to the question *is* simple, and that it is, yes. From the 1560s, when Lawrence Vaux and William Allen began to agitate in Haigh's county, the motto was 'Go ye out'; and it must be a fair bet that, for those who preached going out, and for those who were persuaded to do it, there were more important things than the moral tradition. A recusant is a person who, when the pews are given out, does not put in for one, since to cohabit with the unfaithful is to endanger his immortal, and individual, soul.[15]

At the preaching end, we have Allen's description of the new sort of priest who would be needed to expound the doctrine, and would be trained in the continental colleges. A conditioning was required, to which Jesuit influence largely contributed: the priests were to be *zelanti*. They were to hate heretics, not just heresy; to bewail the calamities of the church as due to the backsliding of

---

[13] Robert Frost, 'Mending Wall', in C. Day Lewis (ed.), *Robert Frost: Selected Poems* (London, 1955), p. 33; Ingram, *Church Courts*, p. 111.

[14] Christopher Haigh, 'The Continuity of Catholicism in the English Reformation', *Past and Present*, no. 93 (1981), p. 45.

[15] Nick Alldridge, 'Loyalty and Identity in Chester Parishes', in Wright, *Parish, Church and People*, p. 98.

Catholics; to repent, and to be converted; to be ready to save souls by a new way of life – activist, steeped in pious emotions, ready for martyrdom. If moral tradition surfaced anywhere in Allen's prescription, it was perhaps in his reference to the less brilliant products of his college ('because Mercury cannot be made of every log'), who could be sent off to 'uplandish places, where there is no other better learned than themselves, to hear the common Catholic people's confession' and, I suppose, enquire about the deadly sins. Durandus's *Rationale* was not a set book at Douai or Reims.[16]

The early practitioners of this 'spiritual workmanship' do not suggest that reconciling disputes was one of their interests. References to it are few, and dampening, especially among the Jesuits. There is one from Robert Parsons, writing from London in 1581: 'Quarrels between Catholics on any matter are almost unheard of: if any difference of opinion takes place, as a rule it is submitted entirely to the direction of the priests.' Parsons, we may gather, was insensitive to the moral tradition and an exceptionally bad prophet besides. The missionary autobiographies of John Gerard and William Weston indicate that they had no time for it, between converting and exorcising, giving the Spiritual Exercises, escapology and reforming the households of the gentry. The Jesuit disciple Mary Ward composed for her followers a version of the Jesuit 'institute' in which she changed the duty of reconciling enemies ('reconciliatio dissidentium') to that of 'reconciling those dissenting from the church'. In Ireland, where there was a heavy demand for priests to deal in peacemaking, the Jesuit superior Christopher Holywood, who seems to have taken Henry Garnet as his model, told his members to steer clear of it,

---

[16] T. F. Knox (ed.), *Letters and Memorials of William Cardinal Allen* (London, 1882), pp. 62–7, 32–4. Hating heretics is an addition of 1580 to an original of 1578 which only required 'zeal and just indignation' against them 'as far as the Lord permits'.

as detrimental to their spiritual mission. As the Sarum rite was superseded by the Roman, the *pax* ritual disappeared from the mass. In 1625 an old lady on the Isle of Eigg, who had been alive under the old regime, commented critically on the point to two Franciscan missionaries; they fobbed her off.[17]

Priests would not have expected this kind of feedback from the pious gentry of southern England, to whom the new devotion of frequent confession and communion came more naturally than the annual social communion of tradition. This was not simply because of their restricted circumstances: it chimed with the rise of a domestic piety among them which, Colin Richmond tells us, had already in the fifteenth century encouraged a 'privatisation' of their religious practice. Christopher Haigh very properly remarked that the piety of the recusant household was largely a fifteenth-century piety; and I was struck, in reading Richmond, to find the portable altar, which I had ignorantly taken to be an invention of the missionary priests, widely diffused for domestic mass in the fifteenth century.[18]

So it was not just danger and secrecy which inhibited the Elizabethan and early Stuart Catholic mission from embodying the moral tradition, and gave it a drift very different from that of Watson, or Gilpin, and the Marian church. But lest I seem to be offering a dossier rather than a narrative, I must concede that

[17] Parsons, in Catholic Record Society, XXXIX (1942), p. 86; P. Caraman, *Autobiography of John Gerard* (London, 1959 edn), p. 180, about a duel, is the only remotely relevant thing; Mary K. Stevenson, 'Mary Ward's Adoption of the Jesuit Rule in the Context of the Catholic Reformation' (John Carroll University, University Heights, Ohio, MA thesis, 1996), p. 41 (many thanks to Ms Stevenson for sending me a copy); E. Hogan, *Ibernia Ignatiana*, I (Dublin, 1880), pp. 164–5, and my 'The Counter-Reformation and the People of Catholic Ireland, 1596–1641', in T. D. Williams (ed.), *Historical Studies*, VIII (Dublin, 1971), pp. 158–9; C. Giblin (ed.), *The Irish Franciscan Mission to Scotland, 1619–1646* (Dublin, 1964), p. 66.

[18] Colin Richmond, 'Religion and the 15th Century English Gentleman', in Barrie Dobson (ed.), *The Church, Patronage and Politics in the 15th Century* (Gloucester and New York, 1984), pp. 193–208; Haigh, 'The Continuity of Catholicism', pp. 66, 69.

after the decades of emergency, as something like regular con-
gregational life began to reappear among recusant Catholics,
the moral tradition popped up again. There is the case of the
Benedictine Ambrose Barlow, settled at Leigh in Lancashire and
executed in old age in 1641. He had chosen to live in a farmhouse,
not with the gentry; his mode of life was demotic, some said
clownish, going about in slippers and a floppy hat; he had 'a great
talent', we are told, in peacemaking, and his Easter communions
were feasts of hospitality. He was not all geniality, since he was
known to be a 'rigid' confessor, but he was a model which probably does, as Haigh suggests, indicate in much of Lancashire a
continuity in the moral tradition which the new clergy of the
Church of England were unable to divert.[19] It may well be that
Barlow, as a Benedictine, was more of a traditionalist than his
Jesuit colleagues; but we also find seventeenth-century Jesuits
preaching on peace and settling disputes. True, this comes from
their Annual Letters, of which anyone ought to be wary; but at
Little Crosby, where the priest was usually a Jesuit, we find a
string of reconciliations between members of a well-rooted and
perhaps not over-zealous congregation done by the landlord
(Nicholas Blundell), the priest (his friend Robert Aldred), both
of them together, a committee of priests or a visiting bishop.[20]
They date from the early eighteenth century, by which time the
secular clergy had produced a very respectable exponent of the
pastoral career in the Presbyterian convert John Gother. Gother
had evidently thought about the moral tradition: he had surely
read Herbert and Baxter, and knew the Prayer Book, from which

---

[19] See my *English Catholic Community* (London, 1975), p. 265, and index under name;
Haigh, 'The Continuity of Catholicism', p. 45.

[20] H. Foley (ed.), *Records of the English Province of the Society of Jesus* (7 vols. in 8,
London, 1875–83), vii/2, pp. 1104, 1106, 1114; F. Tyrer (ed.), *The Great Diurnall
of Nicholas Blundell* (Record Society of Lancashire and Cheshire, 3 vols., 1968–72), i,
pp. 46, 83, 107, 161, 188, ii, p. 147.

he borrowed. But perhaps the French Oratorians were the main influence on him and his instructional-cum-liturgical mode; he gives a strong impression of wanting to revise the traditional *topos* for another age. He said that a priest should procure the peace of his congregation at the expense of his own, acting as a lightning-conductor for their aggressions 'by those unwelcome truths which his duty obliges him to speak'. The laity at mass should skip their private devotions to offer the sacrifice with the priest, and when he spread his hands over the chalice at the *Hanc igitur*, and prayed to God 'to dispose our days in thy peace', they ought to say to themselves: 'Behold, O Lord, we all here, though of different conditions, yet united by Charity as members of that one Body, of which thy dear Son is head, present to thee, in this Bread and Wine, the symbols of our perfect Union.'[21] We can see a shift from charity between individuals to charity between classes; a shift, in the mass, from the pre-communion to the pre-consecration; a shift from the action to the thought. We also observe a certain lack of warmth all round: Gother's is not an unsocial mass, but it is a mass for a civil society.

I come to the church papists, and to Alexandra Walsham's recent book on them: a triumph, if I may say so, of youth over age. She says that church papists were important people who have been downplayed for sectarian purposes by previous writers coming from the stable of 'recusant history'. Too true, and *mea culpa*. She holds, positively, that they existed not in a muddle but in a stable state of 'semi-separation' in, rather than from, the Church of England. Since they cannot all have squeezed into the recusant body most of them, or of their successors, will have

---

[21] [John Gother], *Instructions and Devotions for Hearing Mass* ([London], 1740), pp. 9, 63, 73; my *English Catholic Community*, pp. 132, 265; Eamon Duffy, 'Joseph Berington and the English Cisalpine Movement' (Cambridge University PhD thesis, 1973), p. 23 – priests not to admit to the sacraments those who had 'openly profess'd an aversion to one another'; on the decline of the *pax*, le Brun, *Explication de la Messe*, I, pp. 583–97.

passed from semi-separation to unseparation, providing sub-stance for the parish Anglicanism of Christopher Haigh or the traditionalised Prayer Book religion of Eamon Duffy. Let us suppose that this story about church papists is also true.[22] My business here must be to enquire whether their containment within the Church of England, their failure to answer the call to come out, was due to a stronger feeling about the moral tradi-tion than can have prevailed among recusants. Recusants, from time to time, gave as their reason for not communicating, and perhaps for not going to church at all, that they were 'out of charity': can we suppose that non-recusants' motive for conform-ity was a wish or sense of obligation to be 'in charity' with their neighbours?[23]

Tightly construed, the hypothesis would apply to communic-ants only, not to simple church-attenders; but the motive might be attributed in either case. A communicant, we might say, would be a Catholic who thought communion a social rite expressing peace and unity, and found the Prayer Book service adequate to the purpose; a non-communicant someone who thought com-munion an act of devotion, but wished to fulfil the obligation of charity so far as possible. It looks a plausible idea. I see that I have attributed the motive myself, and the general proposal would accord well enough with the drift of these lectures, especially of the last. I am afraid that I must, reluctantly, be something of a wet blanket about it. The Lutheran analogy is probably misleading. The Church of England was a great deal less traditional than the Lutheran churches; and I do not have the impression that one of their great attractions, communion in both kinds, cut much ice in

---

[22] Alexandra Walsham, *Church Papists: Catholicism, Conformity and Confessional Polemic in Early Modern England* (Woodbridge, Suff., 1993), pp. 5 and *passim*; Haigh, *English Reformations*, p. 291; Duffy, *Stripping of the Altars*, p. 589.

[23] Walsham, *Church Papists*, pp. 86 and n. 63, 96, citing the well-known 'character' of the church papist by John Earle, 1628; my *English Catholic Community*, pp. 121–4.

England. Until the seventeenth century at least, the atmosphere in Germany was roughly consensual; the atmosphere in England was and remained tense.

So far, there does not seem to be much evidence from the grass-roots to support the idea, and George Gifford, on his own, will not do. The polemical literature proves a blank. All sorts of motives for church-going are canvassed: fear, expense, obedience and loyalty, preservation of place, saving one's strength for the future, the pleas of weeping wives and children. Nobody defends it, or says that somebody else defends it, as an act of charity: as it were, that 'rational charity' which Dr Walsham has evoked in speaking of semi-separatism. It is true that the Elizabethan controversy was almost wholly about the gentry and nobility: from the recusant side, there was a lot about the 'scandal' which great or relatively great church-goers would be giving to their inferiors. But after 1603, when we are told that writers were more interested in the lower orders, we still do not seem to find anything about charity.[24] We do find, from the missioners' books of cases of conscience, among the problems of travelling gentlemen and so on, that somebody has enquired whether it was all right to take part in rush-bearings or the decoration of churches for feast days. The answer was yes in the first case, and no in the second; it is a pity nobody asked about church-ales. We may also have a suspicion that, when he harped on the textbook point that church-going was an act of 'schism' and a sin against the peace and charity of the true body of Christ, a defender of strict recusancy like Henry Garnet was indicating that in real life a dread of schism worked to

---

[24] Walsham, *Church Papists*, pp. 32ff, 57, 69, 94, 25; for 'rational charity', Patrick Collinson, *Godly People* (London, 1983), p. 533, though the charity here is to other members of a separated church. Henry Garnet, *A Treatise of Christian Renunciation* (1593: repr. Menston, Yorks., 1970), p. 53 and *passim; idem, An Apology against the Defence of Schisme* (1593: repr. Menston, Yorks., 1973), pp. 85–108.

the opposite effect.[25] Perhaps he was; but a speculation like this will hardly do more for us than George Gifford's intelligent fiction.

Unable to bring any message from the grass-roots, I offer you what I have, which comes from the opposite direction. If we are to take church papists seriously, we shall have to deal with a man who must in the end find his niche as the most eminent of them. I mean Lord Henry Howard. Second son of the poet and Protestant earl of Surrey, brother of the fourth duke of Norfolk executed for treason in 1572, he was the principal ornament of his house from then until the reign of James I, when he achieved power as earl of Northampton. He was a courtier of Queen Elizabeth, who on the whole admired and protected him: her chapel was the parish church to which, we are told, he went when she was looking. He was extremely learned, and shares with George Herbert the distinction of having been reader in rhetoric in Cambridge. He left a vast corpus of writings: published works in defence of the Elizabethan regime, conservatively interpreted; unpublished writings which expose his private meditations, his devotional and theological concerns. He was certainly a Catholic in his maturity: he differed from the Church of England about the sacraments, and did not hold with justification by faith; perhaps a Henrician Catholic, since he appears to have ascribed no authority, spiritual or temporal, to the pope. As a person he has not appealed to posterity: 'proud, pedantic and cynical', envious and vindictive, says the historian of his Jacobean career. Was he, nevertheless, a voice for the moral tradition?[26]

[25] P. J. Holmes (ed.), *Elizabethan Casuistry* (Catholic Record Society, LXVII, 1981), pp. 25, 110; Walsham, *Church Papists*, p. 29.
[26] Linda Levy Peck, *Northampton: Patronage and Policy at the Court of James I* (London, 1982), chap. 1 and pp. 7, 111–12, 188–9, 213ff; my *Giordano Bruno and the Embassy Affair* (London, 1991), index under name. There is also the case of the common lawyer Edmund Plowden, a conscientious church papist and a very active arbitrator:

For the time being, I cite one or two things in his favour. I take it that he thought, as against Garnet, that the authority of the pope was now, in England, unthinkable as a guarantee of peace and unity; and that Elizabeth's supremacy was an infinitely better bet. About the lower echelons of the church we can find something of what he thought in his defence of the Elizabethan regime against Thomas Cartwright. Cartwright had objected against the intermeddling of bishops in civil causes. Howard responded:

> As for dealing in civil causes, so far as they are annexed and coherent to a spiritual function, maintaining peace and keeping quiet in the country, I think it very profitable and requisite for every state, and no slender furtherance to that making of atonement, whereunto Christ hath promised so great reward ['Blessed are the peacemakers'].[27]

Here peacemaking keeps its transcendental character: would Archbishop Grindal, peacemaker as he was, have used the word 'atonement', much less spoken of 'reward'? In the see of York, which he is thought to have coveted, Howard would have had more chances of putting ideals into practice than he, or for that matter Grindal, actually had. I do not suppose that in that office his hostility to forward Protestants would have evaporated. Yet in so far as it was a state of personal enmity, it ought to have done. In his public difficulties his recourse was private prayer, and he told himself that before we pray we must remit injuries. This was directly scriptural, like all his meditations; it was indirectly scriptural in that he held that prayer was a form of sacrifice, and before we sacrifice we must be reconciled to our brother, leaving our gift

G. de C. Parminter, *Edmund Plowden* (Catholic Record Society, monograph series 4, 1987), pp. 83, 106–7; as arbitrator, pp. 44, 75, 128, 139–40.

[27] *A Defense of the Ecclesiastical Regimente in Englande* (London, 1574), p. 114. He defends the royal supremacy here, but perhaps would not have done after 1576, when he formally reconverted to Catholicism: my 'English Catholics and the French Marriage, 1577–1581', *Recusant History*, 5 (1959), p. 12.

at the altar if need be. It was in accordance with the Paternoster
doctrine that the forgiving of enemies is the condition of our salvation. I bow to the common opinion that when he was in power
this doctrine went by the board: perhaps by then he had ceased to
pray. But I do not think that either of the passages I have quoted
was a cliché at the time he wrote it (1574, 1584). Both of them
point to a frame of mind which was Catholic but not counter-
reformation: the first not Borromean, the second a world away
from the Spiritual Exercises and those they formed. Howard's
meditations, and his rhetorical prayers, look like an attempt to
adapt the traditional posture to an age of scriptural humanism. He
was no Herbert; but the two of them did share a conviction that
the Temple could not be built while there were wars in the land.[28]

I come, at the end of these lectures, to a question hitherto
postponed, and one of the most delicate I shall have to broach.
At the risk of muddling the history of the Church of England by
severing a branch from its native trunk, I ask: Were the godly, or
self-consciously Calvinist among the English clergy vehicles of
the moral tradition? We see that such ministers cultivated, or had
cultivated for them, a reputation as peacemakers; and this may
well have come as a surprise. We had thought, perhaps, that like
the Jesuits they came to bring not peace but a sword: that they set
parishes by the ears, examined communicants more intrusively
than they liked, excommunicated more freely, separated the
sheep from the goats, kept communion for their friends. Was this
right? It is cheeky of me to seek to answer a question with which
Patrick Collinson has been grappling for decades; but I should be
a coward not to make the effort.[29]

---

[28] Durham University Library, Howard MSS 5, fols. 1–4, 41ᵛff, 50ᵛ; Mark 11.25; Matthew
5.23; 3 Kings (so Douai; Authorised Version 1 Kings) 5.3.
[29] From *The Elizabethan Puritan Movement* (London, 1967), pp. 346–55, *via* 'The Godly',
in *Godly People*, pp. 1–18 (1966), 'Towards a Broader Understanding of the Early
Dissenting Tradition', in *ibid.*, pp. 527–62 (1975), *The Religion of Protestants* (Oxford,

Only a godly survey of the ministry, I should think, could quite complain that such a parson was 'subject to the vice of good fellowship', that such another 'useth to play after a sort the reconciler amongst the simple'.[30] George Gifford's Atheos was a godly satire on the moral tradition. What, then, of the peacemaking prowess of the puritan ministry as expounded in their biographies? Well, we may say: this is like scrumping apples in the autobiographies of the godly, a *topos* the more diligently to be rehearsed as the charge that a godly ministry puts everyone at sixes and sevens appears to be borne out by civil war, king-killing and the mushroom cloud of sectarianisms of the Spirit. This would be a polemical view. If it presupposes in the godly ministry the conviction that 'covenants of peace' were nothing to do with salvation, but something 'merely civil', it can probably be answered by indicating that the only ministers who explicitly took this line were separatists.[31] If it implies that they were more careful to ensure the reign of charity among the faithful than to pursue the hopeless task of diffusing it among the unregenerate, then there may be more to be said for it; the ministers in Dorchester and Northamptonshire who took it as their business to procure 'Christian peace' in a whole town or parish were not the only ones, but sceptics may think they do not quite make the weight.[32]

1982), chap. 6, *The Birthpangs of Protestant England* (London, 1988), chap. 5, to 'The Cohabitation of the Faithful with the Unfaithful', in O. P. Grell *et al.* (eds.), *From Persecution to Toleration* (Oxford, 1991), pp. 51–76.

[30] Collinson, *Puritan Movement*, p. 281.

[31] Collinson, 'Cohabitation', pp. 61, 66; cf. my 'Some Elementary Forms of Durkheim', *Past and Present*, no. 95 (1982), pp. 12, 15. On scrumping, Owen Watkins, *The Puritan Experience* (London, 1972), p. 59.

[32] Felicity Heal, 'The Idea of Hospitality in Early Modern England', *Past and Present*, no. 102 (1984), pp. 84ff; Collinson, 'Towards a Broader Understanding', p. 547; *idem*, 'Cohabitation', pp. 66–7; *idem*, *Puritan Movement*, p. 354; *idem*, *Religion of Protestants*, p. 272.

To see what they may have been thinking we have a number of eminent authors to consult, and I have consulted three of them. William Perkins made a memorable stab at a doctrine of the moral tradition in his *Epieikeia: Or a Treatise of Christian Equity and Moderation* (before 1602; published 1604). The title may make mediaevalists sit up: Perkins drew on Aristotle and Aquinas, as well as on the New Testament, for an account of the Christian virtues of 'peace, neighbourhood [and] true friendship'. 'Where [such peace] is not practised, there is no religion, nor conscience, nor salvation.' 'God forgiveth not a man his faults but upon condition that he shall forgive his brother.' He who says the Paternoster and does not forgive his neighbours condemns himself to eternal punishment. His text was: 'Let your moderation of mind [*otherwise* equity] be known unto all men' (Philippians 4.5); it may not have pleased all his colleagues, or the common lawyers.[33]

Yet as one who believed that the source of real spiritual consolation lay in the doctrine of double predestination, Perkins had to protect his rear. Easy enough, at least in theory, for him to distinguish Aristotelian nature from scriptural supernature: if men do not forgive, it is not possible for the society (fellowship) of men to continue upon earth; but, supernaturally, forgiveness of our brother is not the cause but a sign or effect of our salvation. 'For this is not true, that everyone who forgives is forgiven of God; but this is true, that whoever is forgiven of God will forgive his brother.' Hence the 'shall' in his interpretation of the Paternoster ('*shall* forgive'), which is Luther's: he finds a Pauline text to support him in the predestinarian Ephesians (4.32).[34] The problem with this is that the promise in his text is offered only to the elect:

---

[33] Ian Breward (ed.), *The Work of William Perkins* (Appleford, Berks., 1970), pp. 477–510, at pp. 482, 498, 507.

[34] *Ibid.*, pp. 483, 497, 498–9.

for all his resort to Aristotle and Aquinas, Perkins's grace cannot perfect nature, but must work against it. Are we not to conclude that peacemaking and the forgiveness of trespasses are, for the non-elect, merely human, 'merely civil'? How then can the unregenerate man, in saying the Our Father while not forgiving, condemn himself? He is simply being anti-social, is he not?

In *Epieikeia* these difficulties are kept in hand by Perkins's obvious wish to say for the moral tradition whatever can be said, and even, on his platform, a little more than can be said. In John Rogers's *Treatise of Love* (1629), they come to a head. It contains an exposition of the moral tradition almost as concrete and affectionate as Herbert's. Rogers's love is not discriminatory: 'It's in the plural number, and shewes a communitie, that we must not love one or two or a few, but all'; even if we are to love 'especially all that feare God'. He claimed that 'his loving neighbours of Dedham [had] lived together in peace and unity these twenty-three years'. But soon enough, and a good deal more ringingly than in Perkins, the bell begins to toll. Just as the deadly sins proceed from 'want of faith', so Christian love or charity is a consequence of faith, and those who are not regenerate cannot possess it. It is 'a *sanctified* affection of the heart', to be distinguished from everyday friendliness which is, as the separatists said, 'civil love'. 'Vicinitie and neighbourhood will faile', I quote two of his colleagues, 'but grace and religion will never faile.' Does Rogers have a place, under charity rather than civility, for 'covenants of peace'? What he says about Dedham would make one think so. But even in Dedham many of the people will be 'naughty', and so incapable of making a covenant of peace which is also an act of Christian charity. Rogers may want to fill the gap by falling back, like Borromeo and the Jesuits, on the theory of charity as work: 'Love is a sanctified affection of the heart whereby whosoever is indued withal, endeavoureth to do all the good he can to all.' If so, I think he gets himself into a worse muddle. In peacemaking, which will be required if people are not to avoid communion or to communicate with 'festered hearts', the (hypothetically) regenerate parson or parishioner who promotes the reconciliation will be performing a Christian act, the (perhaps) unregenerate who reconcile themselves will not, which is absurd. I hope it is not unfair to Ralph Josselin, who was a considerable peacemaker among his flock at Earl's Colne in Essex, who did not limit his efforts (though he limited his communion) to the godly few, and who prayed eloquently to the 'prince of peace', to sense that he was a victim of this difficulty.[35]

It seems that predestinarian pastors who made a bid for the moral tradition fell to a sort of Catch 22: the more they sought to embrace it, the more it slipped out of their hands. I am not competent to say whether this is a general rule, but it seems to apply in England. It must be germane to the case of the last of my affectionate English divines, the great Richard Baxter. We can take it from Baxter that he did not become an Arminian; but we can also take it that a 'contented ignorance' about double predestination was all that he thought a Christian faith required. So we may not be surprised to find him quietly pushing his *summa* of practical divinity in the direction of the unreconstructed moral tradition: so far as I can see, he leaves out all the qualifications which had dogged the efforts of his precursors to integrate it with a predestinarian theology. In the essentials, though not in all his practical recommendations, he took Herbert as a model. On forgiveness, God and man's, he came back to the Paternoster. I

---

[35] John Rogers, *A Treatise of Love* (London, 1629), prefatory epistle, pp. 8, 24–8, 38, 76–9, 91, 152–3 (many thanks to Eamon Duffy for telling me about Rogers); cf. Haigh, *English Reformations*, pp. 287–8 (Perkins); Collinson, 'The Godly', p. 4 (Dedham); *idem*, 'Towards a Broader Understanding', p. 547 (quoting Dod and Cleaver on 'vicinitie'); Alan Macfarlane (ed.), *The Diary of Ralph Josselin, 1616–1683* (London, Records of Social and Economic History, new series III, 1976), pp. 233, 276, 278, 457, 563 and *passim*.

guess he was too much of a scripturalist or Calvinist to revive the mediaeval doctrine of the Incarnation as a universal *pax*; but he did restore something transcendental to the notion of peace. 'Pride is the gunpowder of the mind, the family, the church and the state: it broke the Peace between God and the apostate Angels.' 'He that is not a son of Peace is not a son of God.' It has been tempting to suppose that his whole vocation as a peacemaker was absorbed by the urgency of restoring the peace of the English church; but he told his parishioners at Kidderminster 'above all [to] see that you be followers of Peace and Unity, both in the Church and among yourselves'. And where the empirical division of the godly and the ungodly had tied Perkins and Rogers into theological knots, it evoked in Baxter the untheological response of adding to the deadly sins the sin of censoriousness. The faithful were to avoid 'a sour singularity in lawful things'; to 'come as near [your honest neighbour] as you can'. Censoriousness is 'a Vermine which crawleth in the carkas of Christian love', and the cause of England's troubles: 'religious and moral invidiousness', Patrick Collinson nicely calls it.[36] With Baxter's distinguished act of restitution, and his unconviction, as I take it, about predestinarian doctrine, I leave the history of the moral tradition in the England of the Post-Reformation.

That makes four stories: all different, like stamps, and all the same, like turnips. I shall not retell them now: synopsis has her niche at the beginning of things, not at the end. It is time to try and fathom to what single drama, *mythos* or plot they may contribute. Whatever it may be, it will surely be one of the larger spectacles of the Post-Reformation; it has also turned out to be a spectacle of

---

[36] Richard Baxter, *The Christian Directory. The 4th Part: Christian Politicks* (London, 1677 edn), pp. 50, 89ff, 91, 229ff, 235–6, 272ff; Geoffrey Nuttall, *Richard Baxter* (London, 1965), pp. 4, 10 (Herbert), 45, 64–5, 111, 120–1; Collinson, 'Cohabitation', p. 73.

considerable length. If we had thought, as we might have done if we had started with the history of the word 'charity' in the post-reformation age, that what I have called the moral tradition disappeared in the upheavals of the sixteenth century, or indeed in the piety of the fifteenth, we shall have to think again. It may be virtually axiomatic that a tradition is in decline, but this is another word we shall have to use with care. What exactly is it that we think was declining? Is it the practice of peacemaking in connection with the rites and obligations of Christianity; or is it the religious sense that peacemaking is holy, transcendant of this-worldly doings and something intimately to do with the condition of the universe as witnessed to by the coming of Christ? They are different things.

In either sense, though more readily in the first than the second, we might well conclude that during the Post-Reformation the moral tradition was not waning but waxing. It would depend on what we thought about its status in pre-reformation Christianity, which I have simply assumed. I say 'pre-Reformation Christianity', not 'the pre-Reformation church', since one was not identical with the other, though it was not its opposite either: the distinction is particularly worth making in Italy, where the moral tradition had a special force. If my assumption is unsound then the story might be read as a marvellous flowering, which in some degree it surely is. More generally acceptable, I imagine, would be the notion that things were probably much the same before and after; which might imply that my moral tradition is so universal that there is nothing really to be said about it except that it is always going on. I confess that now I have finished these lectures I have rather more sympathy for this point of view than I had when I began to think about them. But I fancy we can do a little better.

We have seen various instances, in various times and places, of what looks like a general story. In the onset of reform, by which we can agree to mean a general shake-up of parochial life done with good intentions, the moral tradition is shaken with it, because moral authorities mistrust it as sloppy, unzealous and time-wasting, and think there are more urgent things to be doing. We might have thought that this was a permanent effect, to be identified perhaps with a passage in the moral system from the deadly sins to the Ten Commandments. It now appears more likely that the effect was temporary, and as things settled down the moral tradition (and the deadly sins?) re-emerged vigorously, like the return of the repressed. We can say rather firmly that the repression was as much part of the Catholic story as of the Protestant, and the return perhaps more vigorous among Protestants than among Catholics. It is possible that on both sides the tradition when it returned was rather more a speciality of the various types of ministry, rather less the possession of a relatively unsegregated *Christianitas*, than it had been before; but I would not put too much money on that horse.

When we have digested the vigour of its return among Protestants, we need to enquire what was the effect upon the moral tradition of Protestantism as such: its theology, its new forms of church order, its practice. Of Reformation practice, I am sure we ought to say that a revitalisation of Christian feelings, their more immediate refreshment at the sources, or simply the jolt ministered to them by the upsetting of customary ways, were influences giving a boost to the historic practices of charity. Reformation theology is another matter. The moral tradition had heavy contractual implications, to which the Paternoster and the Vulgate *Gloria* gave authority: to that extent it appeared incompatible with justification by faith alone. That doctrine will have had some effect in weakening the sense that the greatest of these was charity; those, from Luther to Perkins, who tried to turn tradition round by arguing that charity was a necessary consequence of faith always give me an impression of special pleading.

Problems about the sacraments seem surmountable; this one nagged away persistently. It became more knotty as double predestination was widely held to be the proper interpretation of justification by faith. Followers of Calvin (or was it Beza?) became obsessed with the idea that peace on earth, even or especially in the reformed version ('goodwill toward men') was a text giving authority to universal salvation.[37] At the same time their reinvention of the church appears to have made peace among the faithful a more pressing requirement than before. They were, it seems, in a cleft stick from which only departure from predestination, handing peace on earth over to the state or sectarianism could rescue them: in England they ended up with all three. Might we say that among Lutherans and other English Protestants, the story is about the return of the repressed; among the Reformed, about the relapse of the revived?

Beneath their feet, and the feet of all our participants as they stood on the promontory of the Post-Reformation, we can see a current eroding, a good deal more radically than reformation theology, the banks of the moral tradition. 'Something more subtle, more deeply burrowing under foundations': I quote Evennett, who meant scepticism and rationalism. What I have to mean is the current of civility, pulling towards the achievement of 'civil society', with either size of 's'. Civil society, in one sense, is the opposite of barbarousness; in another, it is the opposite of Christian society (small 's'), which is what I have been talking about. The oppositions are not so distinct as one might immediately suppose. Invented, for our purposes, by the Renaissance, precipitated by the wars of religion, civil society

---

[37] *The Geneva Bible* (facsimile of 1560 edn, intro. by Lloyd E. Berry: Madison, Wis., 1969), New Testament, fol. 27^v, has a note on 'towards men good will' in Luke 2.14: 'The fre mercie and goodwil of God, which is the fountaine of our peace and felicity, and is chiefly declared to the elect.'

must be the real terminus of the moral tradition, so far as it has one.[38]

That tradition depended for its persuasiveness on the force of personal, face-to-face, eyeball-to-eyeball enmity, as a formal and public condition, among the peoples of the West. I presume that that force was gently in decline. *Pax* would, as Giovanni Maria Visconti wanted, be translated into *tranquillitas*. Ours, for the moment, not to reason why: if we are gripped by the connection between banditry and the moral tradition among the Italians we shall instantly look to the law, the state and the police. Perhaps too instantly: no one will wish to be caught dating the death of God to the diffusion of the fire-engine.[39] Let us leave that as none of our business: it *is* our business to envisage the consequences for the history of Christianity of a general devaluation of the moral tradition which we should expect to ensue from a tranquillisation of the world. Post-reformation Christianity was mostly a Christianity of established churches, which have provided most of my matter. The drift of these lectures, I confess, has been towards insinuating that these churches secured or retained the loyalty of their populations by proving themselves fit vessels of the moral tradition. If that were so, it would follow that a decline of this tradition would go some way towards accounting for a decline of Christianity in the West.

[38] Evennett, *Spirit of the Counter-Reformation*, p. 24; my 'Some Elementary Forms of Durkheim', pp. 8–16.
[39] Thomas, *Religion and the Decline of Magic*, pp. 17–20, 782–3 for the fire-engine, but *not* for the thought.

INDEX

Acquaviva, Claudio, Jesuit 64
Agulhon, Maurice 39
Albert V, duke of Bavaria 59
Aldred, Robert, Jesuit 85
Aleria, Corsica, diocese 20
Allen, William, cardinal 82–3
Alsace (Elsass) 61, 66, 67–8, 71
Annecy 37
Antonino Pierozzi, Dominican,
    archbishop, saint 12
Aretino, Pietro 6 and n.
Arnauld, Antoine 44
Austria 59, 62
Avignon 33, 35

Bamberg 70–1
bandits, *banditi* 18, 21–2 and n., 25n.,
    64
Barlow, Ambrose, Benedictine 85
Bavaria 59–60, 61–3, 68
Baxter, Richard 74, 85, 95–6
Bergamo 16
Bernardino of Siena, Franciscan, saint
    5, 17, 57
Bérulle, Pierre de 41
Beza, Theodore 99
Blundell, Nicholas 85
Bodin, Jean 34
Bollani, Domenico, bishop 22–4
Bologna, archdiocese 21

Bordeaux, archdiocese 38
Borromeo, Carlo, cardinal,
    archbishop, saint 11–18, 19–26,
    29, 36–7, 44–5, 55, 68, 94
Borromeo, Federico, cardinal,
    archbishop 20, 24–6, 37, 79
Bouchard, Gérard 47
Brandenburg 57, 65
Bremond, Henri 36
Brescia, diocese 22
Brigden, Susan 73n., 77
Briggs, Robin 32, 45, 50
Brittany 39, 41, 49–50
Broglia, Carlo, archbishop 19, 24
Brown, Peter 12
Bruno, Giordano 58
Burali, Paolo, cardinal, bishop 19–20
Burgundy 39
Byrd, William, composer 64

Calvinists, Calvinism 34–5, 46–8, 55,
    65, 77, 91–6, 99
Cambridge, university ix, 80, 89
Canisius, Peter, Jesuit 58, 61, 65
Carpenter, Joanna 77
Cartwright, Thomas 90
Castan, Nicole 50
Catholics, Roman
    Italian 3–29
    French 31–51